MODERN ART

Edited by David Britt

MODERN
ART

Impressionism

to Post-Modernism

Thames & Hudson

Published in paperback in the United States of America in 1999 by
Thames & Hudson Inc., 500 Fifth Avenue, New York, New York 10110

thamesandhudsonusa.com

Reprinted in hardcover 2010

Library of Congress Catalog Card Number 99-70796
ISBN 978-0-500-23841-7

Printed and bound in Slovenia by DZS-Grafik d.o.o.

Contents

Preface

DAVID BRITT

Paul Cézanne – an Impressionist from the early days of the movement, in the 1870s – used a word which showed that he had an idea of his own place in an art-historical process. The word was 'primitive'. 'I shall always', he said, 'be the primitive of the path I discovered.' Renaissance painting, in the account given by its sixteenth-century chronicler Giorgio Vasari, evolved as a technique of representing bodies in a structured context of space and light, from the work of a group of pioneers or 'primitives'. Cézanne's hypothesis, a plausible one, was that an analogous process took place in the nineteenth and twentieth centuries, in the course of a massive swing away from what was left of the Renaissance tradition. The pioneers of that process, proud to be called primitives, could hardly realize that Vasari's beautifully simple evolutionary model was not going to apply, and that the modern era in art was to consist of one wave of 'primitives' after another. Six years after Cézanne's death a group of very different artists, the Futurists, were calling themselves 'the primitives of a completely renovated sensibility'. The ten words ending in 'ism' in the titles of the eight essays in this book are ten out of hundreds that have succeeded each other since the birth of Impressionism.

If art from the third quarter of the nineteenth century to the last quarter of the twentieth is an 'era', corresponding in some way to the era inaugurated by the Renaissance, then this modern era is one that contains a confusing multiplicity of visual styles. The affinities between Fragonard and David are visible to us (if not, necessarily, to the artists concerned); but the affinities between Umberto Boccioni and Gilbert and George are not in any sense apparent to the eye. The link in this case is through the idea of 'Modernism' itself, the name of a dimly understood, but manifestly real, historical shift.

Parts of the picture are already clear. The Impressionists gave great offence by showing what was perceived, rather than what the artist knew ought to be there. Seurat and his successors, who included the Fauves and the Futurists, used this vital freedom to show a new kid of *perceived* image: hieratic, dynamic, or transcendental, but always expanding the possible versions of the world of perception. The quasi-scientific idea of a solid world 'out there' – atoms like billiard balls – was something that artists were the first to modify; and the last century and a quarter shows them constantly striving to alter the perceptions of the rest of us. The bafflement that has greeted many of their efforts has much to do with the infinity of alternative universes that they present. 'An object has not one

Henri Matisse
Nude with a Tambourine 1926

1 *Impressionism*

BERNARD DENVIR

Impressionism is the most important thing that has happened in European art since the Renaissance, the visual modes of which it supplanted. From it virtually all subsequent developments in painting and sculpture have stemmed, and its basic principles have been reflected in many other art forms. For a conceptual approach, based on ideas about the nature of what we see, it substituted a perceptual one, based on actual visual experience. For a supposedly stable reality, it substituted a transient one. Rejecting the idea that there exists a canon of expression for indicating moods, sentiments and arrangements of objects, it gave primacy to the subjective attitude of the artist, emphasizing spontaneity and immediacy of vision and of reaction. Formulating a doctrine of 'realism' which applied as much to subject matter as to technique, it eschewed the anecdotal, the historical, the romantic, concentrating on the life and phenomena of its own epoch. Escaping from the studio, the Impressionists laid great emphasis on painting in the open air, in emotional contact with the subject which was engaging their attention. When painting in this way – and even in the studio, when the necessity to capture the *impression* of the subject they were painting was equally dominant – they evolved a technique dictated partly by the haste demanded, partly by the necessity to achieve perceptual reality. They eliminated black shadows and outlines which do not exist in nature; shadows were painted in a colour complementary to that of the object. They used a rainbow palette and experimented with various techniques of broken colour.

Impressionism was one of the first art movements to be linked with a self-conscious group; its practitioners held a number of exhibitions and intermittently acted in unity. But in fact they were very different in their personalities and in their art; it is dangerous to dramatize their achievements by seeing them merely as idealistic revolutionaries reacting against an artistic establishment. That they seemed occasionally to be so was not integral to their achievement, and has little to do with their status as the first modern artists.

Impressionism was born in a certain social and cultural context, which was responsible for shaping its forms and determining its ideology. Most of its practitioners had grown up under the not so distant shadow of the Revolution and of Napoleon; they themselves lived through '48, the Coup d'Etat, the Second Empire, the Franco-Prussian War and the Commune, dying under the Third Republic. The background to their lives was one of constant political turmoil, with which they were necessarily involved.

Auguste Renoir
Moulin de la Galette 1876 (detail)

Mostly they were committed, with varying degrees of intensity (Pissarro was probably the most politically aware, and he was more of an anarchist than anything else), to the left. But whether they wanted to or not, the temper of the times identified them with it: to be a revolutionary in art was to be a revolutionary in everything, and the denigratory adjectives which their enemies chose to describe their work showed that this was taken to include morality as well as politics.

The enemies of the Académie were inevitably enemies of the Establishment, and though none of them professed the bellicose sentiments of Courbet, they were all suspect. By the middle of the century an implicit alliance had been established between Bohemia and the Left – an alliance which, as the events of 1968 proved, subsists into the late twentieth century. Those who fail to comprehend a new art style see in it a threat not only to society, but also to the inner certainties of the ego.

There was not much that was subversive in the personal lives of the Impressionists; on the whole they were pillars of domestic rectitude. And it would be entirely wrong to visualize them, even in their purely professional context, as indolent dependents on the whims of creativity or the fluctuations of inspiration. Their output was prolific – sometimes even unfortunately so. They rose early and set off, their easels on their backs, through the countryside, along the banks of the Seine, or through the streets of Paris, looking for suitable sites, likely landscapes, appropriate scenes. Or they laboured in their studios as long as the light lasted.

They were sensitive to public reaction and did all they could to manipulate it in their favour. They were, almost without exception, anxious to be successful, in the most traditional, conventional way.

They grew up in the Paris of Balzac and came to maturity in the Paris of Zola, seeing its transformation under the guidance of Baron Haussmann from an archaic tangle of great palaces and untidy warrens into the luminous city of broad boulevards, luxurious hotels and verdant parks which, by choosing them so frequently as the subject matter of their paintings, they were to immortalize. For, despite the obvious evils of the nineteenth century, its latter half saw an immense improvement in the amenities of life, and nowhere was this more apparent than in the French capital. Life was easier for a large number of people than ever it had been. Social intercourse was more relaxed, and though cafés, for instance, had always played some part in the cultural life of Paris, in the nineteenth century they assumed a significance which they have never since lost. They provided an invaluable meeting-place for men of similar ideas, where the most fruitful and significant forms of contact could be established, theories propounded, programmes worked out. Cafés were of seminal importance in the creation of artistic groups – and it must not be forgotten that such groups were a comparatively new phenomenon in art, peculiar to the nineteenth century (but not of course to France, as the Nazarenes and the Pre-Raphaelites prove). The history of French art during most of the nineteenth century could be written in terms of cafés: the Brasserie Andler, where Courbet used to preside; the Café Fleurus, with panels decorated by Corot and others; the Café Taranne, patronized by Fantin-Latour and Flaubert; the Nouvelle-Athènes, where Manet, Degas, Forain and Lamy were often to be found; the Café Guerbois, which more than any other place could claim to have been the birthplace of Impressionism.

These changes in the landscape of French and especially Parisian life were closely linked to social changes. The industrial revolution generally, and in particular the real-estate boom in Paris consequent upon the policies of Napoleon III, had created an immense amount of new wealth, most of it possessed by newcomers to affluence. Unversed in the older traditions of patronage, it was they who were largely responsible for the sudden emergence in the nineteenth century of the art dealer. Till then art dealing had been a haphazard business, more highly developed, for historical reasons, in Holland than elsewhere. But by the 1860s a new breed had emerged in all the European capitals. Housed in prestigious premises, able, and indeed eager, to advise and direct both artists and customers, acting as impresario, accountant and public relations officer combined, the dealer provided a new and significant service. He liberated artists from their dependence on the annual official Salon; he opened up new outlets; without him the avant garde would never have existed. This effective influence was especially true for Impressionism, which owes an incalculable debt to the perspicacity, good sense and loyalty of Paul Durand-Ruel and Ambroise Vollard, the movement's main dealers.

The art market was, in fact, expanding at an unprecedented rate – not only because there was more money about. Education was improving; the application of the steam engine to the printing press led to a proliferation of cheap books, and to the emergence of a multiplicity of journals and newspapers. The invention of lithography, the production of cheap chromo-lithographic prints, advances in the techniques of producing line blocks – leading eventually to the application of photographic processes – all produced a growth of visual sophistication and of knowledge not only about the art of the past, but about that of the present. An inevitable concomitant was that much more was written about art than ever before. The art historian and the critic emerged as figures of significance. The latter, of course, was especially important in the context of contemporary art. The public was hungry for guidance, and it is probable that current exhibitions in the Paris of the 1870s received more coverage than they did in Paris of the 1970s. Even hostile criticism was probably better than none, though it is now becoming increasingly apparent that hostility to the Impressionists was by no means universal. The support of Zola, even though based at times on erroneous assumptions, was invaluable.

Further, Impressionism also owed its historical validity to the fact that it reflected the profound changes taking place in the whole of European culture. The colour theories of the polymath chemist Eugène Chevreul (1786–1889) had been published before the Impressionists began to paint, though it would seem that they did not really begin to apply them until the 1880s, in conjunction with associated discoveries made by Helmholtz and Rood. The more significant point is that the scientists and the artists were moving in the same direction, towards a realization that colours were not, as Leonardo and Alberti had believed, immutable realities but depended on individual perception, that they were part of the universe of light, one of the elementary dimensions of nature. Unlike the traditionalists in both fields, the new breed of scientists and artists could

Auguste Renoir
Ambroise Vollard 1902

no longer believe in the existence of a permanent, independent, unchangeable reality which could be controlled by perspective or Newtonian physics – a hypothesis which had done much to allay the anxieties of Western man since the Renaissance.

Unconsciously, they were moving towards a concept of the nature of matter which was to find expression half a century later in the discoveries of Einstein. In this context their concern with time – this is, of course, especially true of Monet, who eventually endeavoured to relate light, time and place in a sequence of serialized images of cathedrals and lily ponds – is especially significant. The advent of the machine, with its fixed temporal rhythms and the demands it made on its users to comply with them, had fostered an obsessive concern with time, symbolized by the vast proliferation of clocks in public places which took place after about 1840, by the emergence of history as a dominant discipline, and by the appearance of systems such as the Darwinian and the Marxist which were essentially time-orientated.

But if time and light were one series of preoccupations which affected the nature of Impressionism, speed, the combination of time and space, was another. Till the popularization of the railway engine in the 1830s and 1840s, nobody had experienced travelling at more than about 15 miles an hour. To see objects and landscapes from a train travelling at 50 or 60 miles an hour emphasized still further the subjective nature of visual experience, underlying the transitory, blurring the precise outlines to which post-Renaissance perspectival art had accustomed the artist's eye, and unfolding a larger, less confined view of landscape. Even the increased ease of transport was significant. The Impressionists opened up the South of France as a source of inspiration; they travelled more extensively than any other group of artists had been able to in the past; their work was nourished by a greater variety of landscape.

There were other technological discoveries of their time which influenced them. Chemistry was extending the range and improving the quality of pigments available to the artist (chemical pigments are purer and more stable than their organic equivalents); paper and other materials were cheaper and generally better. Most important of all, however, was the influence of what had originally been called 'the pencil of nature' – the camera. Its impact on art generally, and on Impressionism specifically, was enormous.

In the first place, the camera then had none of the pejorative 'mechanical' associations with which it was later to be endowed. In 1859 the Salon included a photographic section, and in 1862, after a prolonged legal battle, the courts declared photography an art-form – much to the chagrin of Ingres. His reaction was understandable: the camera was to abrogate one of the, admittedly minor, functions with which artists – especially of his type – had always been entrusted: as documenters of events and appearances; the result, of which the Impressionists must have been half-consciously aware, was to allow painting to be itself, to emancipate it from the necessity of referring to a concept of external reality as an inescapable criterion. Art had achieved a self-sufficiency.

But the Impressionists – and in this they were not unique: many of their more academic contemporaries had come to the same realization –

were aware that photography had made an important contribution to the painter's technical armoury. It enabled him to get a steadier and more continuous look at appearances; it permitted analyses of the nature of structure, and of movement, of a kind which had never been possible before. Photography and the new art were natural allies: the first Impressionist exhibition was held in the premises just vacated by Nadar (Félix Tournachon), photographer, cartoonist, writer and balloonist. Much of Eadweard Muybridge's work in the photographic analysis of movement was carried out in France, where he had worked in collaboration with the painter Meissonier, and it was widely known and discussed in artistic circles. Himself an ardent photographer, Degas saw the publication of Muybridge's instantaneous photographs in *La Nature* in 1878, and thereafter followed his work closely (A. Scharf, 'Painting, Photography and the Image of Movement' in *The Burlington Magazine*, CIV 1962, pp. 186–95), not only being influenced by it in a general way, but making drawings and sculptures from some of the plates in Muybridge's *Animal Locomotion*.

In his work on *Degas, Manet, Morisot*, Paul Valéry summed up some of the perceptual consequences of this new technical 'eye': 'Muybridge's photographs revealed all the mistakes which painters and sculptors had made in depicting, for instance, the movements of a horse. They showed how creative the eye is, elaborating on the data which it receives. Between the state of vision as mere *patches of colour* and as *things* or *objects*, a whole series of mysterious processes take place, imposing order on the jumbled incoherence of mere perception, resolving contradictions, reflecting prejudices which have been formed in us since infancy, imposing continuity, connection, and the systems of change which we classify as *space, time, matter*, and *movement*. That is why the horse was supposed to move in the way the eye seemed to see it, and it might be, if that old-fashioned method of representation was studied with enough percipience, we might be able to discover the *law* of unconscious falsification which enabled people to picture the positions of a bird in flight or a horse galloping, as if they could be studied at leisure.'

Implicit in Valéry's notions are many of the aims and preoccupations of the Impressionists. Moreover, the vision of the camera incorporated that very element of immediate spontaneity which had become such a desideratum. It froze gestures, immobilized a movement in a street, fixed for ever a dancer's pirouette. It conveyed a form of truth: it was real, and the Impressionists were above all else Realists – not only in their choice of subjects from everyday, ordinary life and everyday, ordinary people, but in their determination to be visually sincere, not to vamp up the things they saw, not to paint them as they *thought* they were, but as they actually were. Zola, writing in 1868 about Monet, Bazille and Renoir in his *Salon*, called them *Actualistes*: 'Painters who love their own times from the bottom of their artistic minds and hearts. . . . They interpret their era as men who feel it live within them, who are possessed by it, and happy to be so. Their works are alive because they have taken them from life, and they have painted them with all the love they feel for modern subjects.'

The vision of the camera was an enormous incentive in this direction. And it influenced not only the Impressionists' attitudes but their style.

Time and time again the composition of their paintings imitates, or is influenced by, the arbitrary, unselective, partly random finality of the photograph. No longer is there the academic insistence that the subject should be coherent, complete and seen from a compositionally convenient viewpoint. The unity is now in the painting, and in the elements which compose it. Figures may be truncated, poses awkward and ungainly, movements arrested. Chance has entered into painting, to be controlled, manipulated, but still to retain a dominance which it can never lose.

It would, of course, be absurd to see Impressionism purely as the by-product of social, scientific and historical factors. It was rooted firmly in the stylistic evolution of art. Always we are tempted to over-dramatize history, and though Impressionism was indeed the nucleus of the new and the revolutionary, we see it now as more closely related to the art of its own time than the simplifications of criticism once seemed to demand. The Pre-Raphaelites, for instance, though they adopted a different technique, were equally concerned with visual and social realism; the cult of 'sincerity' was widespread, and had been formulated by Ruskin; the academic Meissonier's light, nervous brush-stroke was not unlike the *facture* of many of the Impressionists in the later 1860s, and round about this period Millet's paintings began to palpitate with a hitherto unfamiliar light.

Though they rejected official art, the Impressionists owed an allegiance to some of their immediate predecessors. Manet's teacher Thomas Couture, though apt to paint pictures of decadent Romans, suggested that artists of the future might find as appropriate themes workers, scaffolding, railways (*Méthodes et entretiens d'atelier*, Paris, 1867, p. 254) and there was a whole tradition – of what might be called potential avant-garde painters – which contributed significantly to the techniques and ideology of Impressionism. Delacroix, with his romantic fervour and liberated attitude towards colour, was an obvious idol. So too was Courbet, who once said 'Realism is Democracy in art', and whose life-style as well as his actual work had a very marked influence, especially on Pissarro and Cézanne.

The real achievement of the Impressionists is that they gave coherence and form to tendencies which had for some considerable time been latent in European art. Turner and Constable, for instance, whose influence is discussed later, had been concerned with many of the same problems about light, colour and the approach to a 'realistic' interpretation of landscape. The whole of the Barbizon school had been painting out of doors (*au plein air*) since the 1840s, even though they usually completed their paintings in the studio. Narcisse-Virgile Diaz (1807–76) had been one of the most forthright opponents of 'the black line' in painting, and his exercises in capturing the effects of sunshine coming through the dark greens of the forest, all expressed in a heavy impasto, contained obvious elements of Impressionism. It was he who, meeting Renoir painting in Fontainebleau, said, 'Why the devil do you paint so black?' – a remark which had an immediate effect on the younger artist's palette – and who, incidentally, allowed Renoir to buy painting materials on his account. Théodore Rousseau (1812–67), who expressed the ideal 'always to keep in mind the virgin impression of nature', carried an interest in the rendering of atmospheric effects to a point where it came close to Monet. The sense of poetry, the compulsion to reproduce scrupulously what he saw, and the light silvery tonality of Corot (1796–1875) had an obvious impact, and the luminous Northern seascapes of Eugène Boudin (1824–98), with their vivacious directness, their creamy impasto and their radiance, made it almost inevitable that, though not an 'official' Impressionist, he should participate in their first group show.

There were other artists outside of France who anticipated Impressionism, or followed similar lines of approach. Outstanding among these are the Germans Adalbert Stifter (1805–68), who was also a poet and stumbled almost accidentally on those qualities of visual sincerity and spontaneity typical of the movement, and Adolf Menzel (1815–1905), whose mastery of light was only appreciated after his death. The Dutchman Johan Jongkind (1819–91) was virtually a Parisian, and though he did not practise *plein-air* painting, he was obsessed with representing in his works not what he knew about the subject, but what appeared to him under certain atmospheric conditions. It is interesting that in an article in *L'Artiste* in 1863, the critic Castagnary said of him: 'I find him a genuine and rare sensibility. In his works everything lies in the *impression* [my italics].'

The art of the past was revealed to painters of the mid-nineteenth century in a way which would have been impossible before. Till the 1840s museums and art galleries were few and far between, but between then and the end of the century they proliferated at an extraordinary rate. Sisley, Monet and Pissarro saw the works of Turner, Constable and others in London's National Gallery, which was then only a few decades old. Every provincial city of importance acquired its cultural institutions, and, in ever-increasing numbers, works of art which had once belonged to private collectors found their way into public collections, where they were described and analysed by critics as perspicacious as the painter Eugène Fromentin and others. It was through these innovations that the Impressionists became conscious of, and reacted to, a whole range of old masters, from the early Renaissance painters to Dutch landscapists such as Ruysdael, all of whom gave sanction to their visual explorations and enlarged their range. The Louvre, of course, had been in existence for some time as a public gallery, and its treasures had been greatly enlarged by Napoleon. But even here an important innovation took place in the 1830s, under the reign of Louis-Philippe, when in consequence of that monarch's dynastic preoccupations with Spain, the gallery acquired an important collection of paintings by hitherto little-known artists such as Velázquez, Ribera and Zurbarán, all of whom were to have an enormous impact on the painters of the 1870s. In 1851 Napoleon III reopened the newly rearranged galleries, which had been enhanced by the addition of the Rubens *Medici* cycle. Despite the contrary image of him which has grown up, Napoleon III's administration of the governmental Beaux-Arts department was far more enlightened and progressive than anything else of the same nature in Europe. Special copying facilities were provided at the Louvre, the Palais du Luxembourg was given over to contemporary art, and it was, after all the Emperor himself who initiated the Salon des Refusés in 1863.

Another new set of influences came from outside Europe. As far back as 1856 Japanese art had started to infiltrate into Paris, and six years later Madame Soye, who had lived in Japan, opened a shop, 'La Porte Chinoise', in the Rue de Rivoli; the simple colours and summary treatment of light and shade which were to be seen in the prints of Hokusai and others began to have their effect on a number of artists including Whistler, Rousseau, Degas, and later Van Gogh and Gauguin.

Edouard Manet (1832–83), too, was intrigued and influenced by this revelation from the East, but that is not surprising, for though the accidents of history forced on him the role of the great innovator, and the *maître d'école* of Impressionism, few painters have paid more attention to the art of the past and of their own time. His most famous painting, *Le Déjeuner sur l'herbe* (d'Orsay) of 1863, which when it was exhibited at the Salon des Refusés aroused a storm of ridicule and controversy (which effect may not have been entirely foreign to his intentions), was based on a Giorgione and on a Renaissance print of a painting by Raphael; the equally controversial *Olympia* (d'Orsay) was clearly painted under the direct influence of Titian, and many of his compositional themes were borrowed from his contemporaries, especially Monet and Berthe Morisot. Popular prints also provided for him a frequent repertory of imagery, and the kind of subject he so often chose, rag-pickers, barmaids, actors, crowds enjoying concerts, were the staple of many illustrated magazines of the period. He was an assiduous frequenter of museums in the Low Countries, Austria, Germany and Italy as well as France and Spain, and it was the influence of Velázquez and Goya which informed those of his early paintings – often with the appropriate Hispanic theme – such as *Lola de Valence* (d'Orsay) which had a modest popular success, based on the same wave of public interest in the peninsula which Bizet so successfully exploited in *Carmen*.

Almost in spite of himself, Manet had become to the young artists of the Café Guerbois and the Atelier Gleyre a symbol of revolt, a Robespierre of art. It was his subject matter which appealed at least as much as his free and inventive technique. *Music at the Tuileries*, painted at about the same time as *Le Déjeuner*, emphasized the quality of direct observation of an ordinary urban event, packed though it is with portraits of the painter's friends, and related though it probably is to an engraving of a military band recital which appeared in the magazine *L'Illustration*.

Towards the end of the 1860s, however, Manet began to paint in the open air, and he transferred his attention from exploiting to exploring the effects of light and colour. But he was never entirely to lose the sharp contrasts of light and shade, the sensuous brushwork, the feeling of drama, the flattened volumes which he had derived from the Spaniards, and which are to be seen so vividly present in the *Eva Gonzalès Painting* (National Gallery, London). His sense of the discipline of art persisted despite the freedom which his painting acquired as he came into closer contact with the work of his admirers (he did not participate in the Impressionist exhibitions), especially Monet and Renoir, to whom, paradoxically, he owed so much. This contact was most fruitful between 1874 and 1876 when he worked with them at Argenteuil, where he

Edouard Manet
Le Déjeuner sur l'herbe 1863

Edouard Manet
Olympia 1863

Edouard Manet
Music at the Tuileries 1862

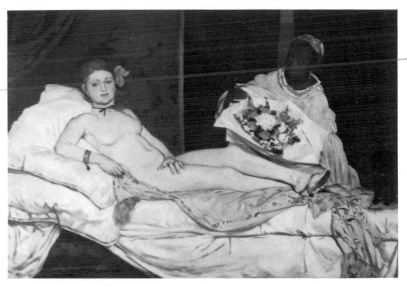

touch. More consistently than any other of his students, she preserved
Corot's silvery iridescence, and it was this quality, allied to an almost
uninhibited and uncontrolled distribution of brush-strokes, which created
her personal style and explains the undoubted influence she was to have
on Manet, exorcizing the darkness and chromatic inhibitions which
characterized his work after the early 1870s. In her *In the Dining Room*
(National Gallery of Art, Washington) of 1884, for instance, the strokes
which make up the door of the cupboard, the maid's apron, the floor and
the glass in the window are virtually free gestures, visual abstractions,
through which shapes and forms emerge as from a mist.

Both as a person and as a painter Claude Monet (1840–1926) was very
different from Manet. Less detached, less diffident, he was committed by
his nature, by economic necessity – and by a kind of professionalism
which, one feels, Manet would have disdained as being not quite *comme il
faut* – to vigorous exploration of the substance and nature of his art.
Perhaps this is what Zola meant: 'He's the only real man in a crowd of
eunuchs' (though that remark, like so many things Zola said about art,
was not really true, even though compelling). A provincial, born in Le
Havre, with ferociously precocious talents, Monet eventually became
more peripatetic than any of his colleagues, and his subject matter covers
a remarkably wide range of places and themes. Boudin and Jongkind had

Berthe Morisot
The Cradle 1873

Berthe Morisot
In the Dining-room 1886

been early influences on him, and though he deferred to Courbet, he did not imitate him. At the studio of Charles Gleyre he met Bazille, Renoir and Sisley, and he subsequently underwent the virtually obligatory experience of Fontainebleau. But though he had produced by this time some three hundred paintings, and had been accepted in the Salon, he was plagued by economic and psychological stress, and at the age of twenty-six tried to commit suicide (the psychological disturbance common to many of the Impressionists has not received the attention it perhaps merits).

It was not, however, until Monet came to London in 1870 that his art really jelled. Although he professed to dislike Turner's 'exuberant romanticism', and denied in later life that Turner had any influence on him, it is impossible not to see in his use of aerial perspective, his treatment of wide reaches of landscape and of sea, even his concern with the transient, amorphous effects of fog, steam and clouds, something of the influence of the English landscape artists. Then there was the actual quality of London's light, which had so intrigued Whistler: mist on the Thames, with the great buildings and bridges swimming out of it; the green reaches of the parks; the constant mutations of atmosphere.

Pissarro explained it well some thirty years later in a letter to Wynford Dewhurst, who was writing a book, published in London in 1904, *Impressionist Painting*: 'Monet and I were very enthusiastic over London landscapes. Monet worked in the parks, whilst I, living at Lower Norwood, at that time a charming suburb, studied the effect of fog, snow and springtime. We worked from Nature, and later on in London Monet painted some superb studies of mist. We also visited the museums. The

Left:

Edouard Manet
Berthe Morisot 1872

Right:

Claude Monet
On the Beach, Trouville 1870

watercolours and paintings of Turner and Constable, the canvases of Old Crome, have certainly had an influence on us. We admired Gainsborough, Reynolds, Lawrence etc., but we were struck chiefly by the landscape painters, who shared more in our aim with regard to *plein air*, light, and fugitive effects. Watts and Rossetti strongly interested us among the modern men. About this time we had the idea of sending our studies to the Royal Academy. Naturally we were rejected' (pp. 31–32).

A visit to Holland, itself part-ancestor of the English tradition, confirmed Monet in his already obvious concern with light and transience, and some encouragement had come from the fact that Durand-Ruel bought his *On the Beach: Trouville*. A fruitful stay at Argenteuil brought him into closer contact with Manet and Renoir, confirming his instinctive belief that Impressionism provided the appropriate framework for his creative intentions. To the exhibition of

Claude Monet
Women in the Garden 1866–67

Claude Monet
Wild Poppies 1873 (detail)

1874, which owed a great deal to his initiative, he sent five paintings – including *Autumn at Argenteuil* and *Bridge at Argenteuil* – and seven pastel sketches. He continued his association with the movement until the fifth exhibition, to which he refused to send anything. In 1876 he began a series of paintings of the Gare Saint-Lazare which, in their subject matter, their luminous treatment of the effects of atmosphere and steam, their lightly adumbrated but unifying structures, may well be thought of as the most 'typical' of all Impressionist paintings.

A steady, persistent worker, independent of the necessity of waiting on 'inspiration', agonizing over every picture he started, Monet found a prop for creativity in serialism, the creation of sets of works all using the same motif; and so virtually stumbled on one of his most original contributions to the language of contemporary art. Quite apart from the technical use of the system, which has been of such value to later painters, he proved

Claude Monet
Autumn at Argenteuil 1873 (detail)

Claude Monet
The Bridge at Argenteuil 1874 (detail)

and emphasized that a whole range of equally 'real' paintings could be made of the same subject, each varying according to the quality of the light and the time of day. At first rather haphazard – as in the *Gare Saint-Lazare* series, and the views of Westminster Bridge – they became more purposeful with the *Poplar* series and that devoted to the façade of Rouen cathedral, culminating in the *Nymphéas* series, the most remarkable attempt art had ever made to paint the passage of time.

Unlike Manet, he paid little attention to the old masters, being influenced rather by his contemporaries. In *Women in the Garden* (1866–67), and even more in later works, he evolved a method of depicting form by accumulating a mass of brush-strokes which are reconstructed and completed by the spectator to produce the effect he is suggesting. This again was a vital new element in art: the realization that the viewer has to participate, that he has to build his understanding of a painting, just as he 'reads' a landscape. This attitude was essential to the future of art. It

Claude Monet
Poplars on the Epte 1891

Claude Monet
Water-lilies: Sunset 1914–18 (detail)

Claude Monet
Gare Saint-Lazare 1877

was only because Monet destroyed the old limited, arbitrary concept of immutable form that the painters of the twentieth century were able to build new visual structures.

Of Alfred Sisley's contributions to the seventh Impressionist exhibition of 1882 Eugène Manet said that they were the most consistently coherent of the whole group, and it would be difficult to pick on a painter more typical of the movement as a whole. Born in Paris of wealthy English parents, Sisley's (1839–99) career was socially and economically almost the exact reverse of that of his colleagues. Encouraged to become a painter by his father, he began his career cushioned by affluence, and his appearance at Gleyre's studio was that of a young dandy. Leaving there in 1863, at the same time as Bazille, Monet and Renoir, he worked with them, exploring the landscape of the forest of Fontainebleau and, like them, concerned himself with the shimmer of light on leaves and the analysis of shadow, painting, with similar fervour, the glades which had bewitched Daubigny and Courbet in the 1850s.

This was to be his familiar, beloved landscape; short visits to Brittany and England (*Molesey Weir*) were the only occasions when he left the Ile-de-France. Nor did he – unlike Renoir – go far beyond a dedication to landscape, nor yet, unlike Monet, concern himself with the transformations effected by time. The figures (as in the magical *Misty Morning*) are perfunctory. These limitations were self-imposed, but their rigour was probably reinforced by his lack of success. Although he succeeded in getting a painting into the Salon of 1866, Sisley was subsequently rejected, a situation compounded in difficulty by the economic ruin of his father as a consequence of the Franco-Prussian war. Poverty was to be his constant irritant; his outstanding virtue, modesty, he cultivated almost to the point of converting it into a vice. Yet he was

Alfred Sisley
Molesey Weir, Hampton Court c. 1874

singularly dedicated to achieving his own, admittedly limited, form of perfection, and his paintings, at their best, have a clarity, a brilliance and a sense of aesthetic honesty which are infinitely compelling. Nobody could better him in achieving the balance between form and the light which irradiates it, so that the one is never dissolved in the other. The transition between water, trees, building and cloud-flecked sky in *Floods at Port-Marly* is symptomatic of his consistent tonal mastery, and the way in which he conveys a sense of almost palpable atmosphere. Remarkable rather for the delicacy of his perception than for the dynamism of his imagination, Sisley frequently manifests a certain dullness of composition, as evinced for instance in the *Canal Saint-Martin*, where the great weight of the barges grouped at the intersection of the horizontal and vertical extreme and mean ratios is mechanically balanced by the two masts accentuating the gap between the distant houses. But the treatment of the

Alfred Sisley
Floods at Port-Marly 1876

Alfred Sisley
Canal Saint-Martin, Paris 1870

Alfred Sisley
Misty Morning 1874

surfaces, the movement of the water, the radiance on the distant roof-
tops, and the texture of the canal wall are all rendered exquisitely. Sisley's
was a kindred spirit to Corot's in the previous generation. The worst that
can be said of him is that his pictorial reticence has been taken as a
prototype by innumerable lesser talents, whose amateur enthusiasms
have found in his paintings the justification for their own creative
inanity.

Linda Nochlin has suggested this most convincingly in relation to *The Bellelli Family* of 1860–62: 'While Bazille, in his representation of the upper middle class, has firmly rejected the aura of sentimentality or nostalgia that sometimes seems inherent in the theme of the family, transforming his subject into a motif modern in both emotional tone and pictorial structure, Degas has gone one step further, making his family portrait *The Bellelli Family* an occasion for the dispassionate and objective recording of subtle psychological tensions and internal divisions in the representation of a refined group from the Italian minor aristocracy. Once again the implications are built into the pictorial structure; there is no meaningful anecdote to serve as the "purpose" of the picture as there is in most contemporary English work representing a family of a similar class in a situation of overt external and internal disruption.'

Edgar Degas
Head of a Young Woman 1867

Right, above:

Edgar Degas
The Bellelli Family 1860–62

Right, below:

Edgar Degas
The Dance Foyer at the Opéra 1872

Far right:

Edgar Degas
The Dance Foyer at the Opéra 1872 (detail)

Few artists have had a keener sense of pictorial structure than Degas. The spontaneity of his works is an illusion – albeit an infinitely satisfying one. Their compositional logic is absolute, and his treatment of reality is always subordinate to the need for total representation. It was here that he parted most decisively from Impressionism, and most clearly showed himself to be a classicist working within a romantic framework. To the first Impressionist exhibition he sent ten paintings, including *The Dance Foyer* (d'Orsay), and continued to show at all the subsequent exhibitions. Impressionism had contributed much to his technical armoury. He had come to it as one dependent, in the tradition of Ingres, on a linear perfection which had been hammered out in his drawing sketchbooks. It gave him a new sense of the value of light as a means of adding volume, vibration and the suggestion of a dimension more profound than that

But all the time something else was fretting him: the oft-repeated desire to create a synthesis of Renaissance discipline and Impressionist truth – to 'redo Poussin after nature', and 'make Impressionism something solid and durable like the Old Masters'. What he really wanted was to organize into a solid structural role all those visual elements which could be rendered truthfully only by Impressionist techniques. A lot of nonsense has been written on this score, and Clement Greenberg's warning is especially relevant: 'The Impressionists, as consistent in their naturalism as they knew how to be, had let nature dictate the over-all design and unity of the picture, along with its component parts, refusing in theory to interfere consciously with their optical impressions. For all that, their pictures did not lack structure; insofar as any single Impressionist picture was successful it achieved an appropriate and satisfying unity, as must any successful work of art. (The over-estimation by Roger Fry and others of Cézanne's success in doing exactly what he said he wanted to do is responsible for the cant about the Impressionists' lack of structure; in its stead the Impressionists achieved structure by the accentuation and modulation of points and areas of colour and value, a kind of

Paul Cézanne
Portrait of Chocquet 1875–77

Paul Cézanne
The Man with a Straw Hat 1870–71

'composition' which is not inherently inferior to or less 'structural' than the other kind.) . . . Cézanne still felt that [the motif] could not of its own accord provide a sufficient basis for pictorial unity; what he wanted had to be more emphatic, more tangible in its articulation and therefore, supposedly, more 'permanent'. And it had to be *read* into nature' (*Art and Culture*, London, 1973, p. 51).

The changes which his art underwent during the next twenty years, and which were to link the world of the Impressionists with the world of Braque, Léger and Ozenfant, were all motivated by his passionate desire to create a new classical syntax with the vocabulary of Impressionism. Sometimes external factors intervened – especially in regard to his landscapes. The change of locale from the small cosy villages of Pontoise to the larger, exaggerated reaches of the South, with its strong all-pervasive light, its great distances apparent to the eye, its chequered fields and intersected mountains, pushed him even farther into a more ruthless investigation of the mechanics of composition than any of his contemporaries had undertaken. He followed two different approaches, which coincide exactly with those Cubism was to use in the first two decades of the twentieth century. In paintings such as *Chestnut Trees at the Jas de Bouffan* (1883) or the *Mont Sainte-Victoire* of the same year, a process of synthesis is adopted: large and small cubes of form and colour are massed together to create the image. In others – and here again the persistent preoccupation with Mont Sainte-Victoire serves as a touchstone – an analytical approach predominates: forms are extracted from what is seen, volume is dissociated at certain dramatic points around which a new structure is formed. The whole canvas is in movement as the tesserae of paint flicker between their surface impression and the image they

Paul Cézanne
Chestnut Trees at the Jas de Bouffan 1885–87

create. In all his landscapes the sense of space is emotive rather than descriptive, so that at the great distances at which he sometimes paints Mont Sainte-Victoire, one can sense, though one cannot see, the intervening areas.

The organization of volumes around a culminating point is very evident in Cézanne's portraits too, such as that of Chocquet (1877), where each part of the sitter is divided into units of coloured volumes which are put together to create the totality of the image. Later, however, especially in the series of *Card Players*, he seemed almost to extend his volumetric passion to Euclidean proportions: each part of each figure is expressed in terms of cylinders or cubes, but the process is never pushed

Paul Cézanne
Quarry and Mont Sainte-Victoire 1898–1900

Paul Cézanne
Mountains in Provence 1886–90

Paul Cézanne
Four Men Bathing

to its logical limits, and the pleats in the clothes, the pipes, the faces, the background have a Courbet-like lusciousness which counteracts the stringency of the modelling. 'If you paint you can't help drawing as you do it', he once said to Emile Bernard, and it is difficult at times not to feel that the whole of his creative outlook was orientated to the still-life, a world which lent itself perfectly to displaying that solidity, that rotundity which so enraptured him. His fruit has the eternal quality of the vegetation in a seventeenth-century nature poem by Herrick or Traherne; but this is because his paintings are autonomous objects, and the elements which constitute them are valid for no reason other than that they are in

Paul Cézanne
The Card Players c. 1885–90

them. The apples and oranges are in the painting; the painting is the apples and oranges.

It was Cézanne more than anybody else who transmuted Impressionism into a mode of vision and a technique which would reach far beyond the limits of the nineteenth century, a fact which has led to a good deal of near-hysterical and certainly uncritical adulation, for, ironically enough, his art has also spawned a vast amount of flaccid academicism quite alien to his own ideas.

Monet neatly summed up the later development of Impressionism in 1880 when he said that what had once been a church was now a school, and as a school it spread rapidly, becoming, in each country it reached, first a suspect revolutionary art form, and then after a few decades a moribund official idiom. And in all cases it was the earliest protagonists of the style who were the most vital. In Germany Max Liebermann (1847–1935) and Max Slevogt (1868–1932); in what is now Yugoslavia Ivan Grohar (1867–1911) and Matej Sternen (1870–1949) were typical of a generation which adapted Impressionist techniques and attitudes to a national style. Whole groups grew up – in Amsterdam, for instance – dedicated to the propagation of the new gospel. With England the links had always been close: there were the influence of Whistler who had been marginally connected with the movement, the writings of George Moore

Paul Cézanne
L'Estaque 1885

Paul Cézanne
The Blue Vase 1883–87

and above all else the fact that from 1865 till 1892 Alphonse Legros –
who although not himself an Impressionist, had been a friend of Manet,
and in close contact with the influences which created the movement –
taught first at what is now the Royal College, and then at the Slade. It
was the latter institution which spawned the New English Art Club,
whose leaders, Steer, Tonks, Orpen, McEvoy and John, were all indebted
to Impressionism for that liberating impulse.

Impressionism in fact had revolutionized art, and indeed the word was
used, admittedly rather loosely, to describe literary and musical
movements. But it was its developers rather than its imitators who were
most vital, and Cézanne was not alone. In 1884 there was founded in
Paris a *Société des artistes indépendants*, most of whose members were self-
consciously dedicated to renovating Impressionism by adding to it the
systematic qualities which they thought it lacked. They set out to provide
a doctrinal framework for future developments which would give light a
structure based on small points of pure colour, applied in such a way as to
fuse when perceived by the beholder. The outstanding figure of
Pointillism was Georges Seurat (1859–91) who had, significantly, studied
under Henri Lehmann, the pupil of Ingres. Always intent on returning to
those schemata which orthodox Impressionism had set out to destroy, he
even went on in the later stages of his career to attempt to devise modes
for expressing emotion and feeling, very much in the same way as the
Carracci had some centuries earlier. His subject matter was resolutely in
the Impressionist tradition – landscapes and popular entertainment – and
his paintings radiate a lyricism which has little apparent connection with
the austere aesthetic ideology they are supposed to exemplify.

It was inevitable that so beguiling a doctrine should attract disciples; in
France Seurat's ideas were followed by artists such as Paul Signac (1863–

Paul Signac
Debilly Footbridge c. 1926

Georges Seurat
Bathing at Asnières 1883–84

1935) Henri-Edmond Cross (1856–1910) and Maximilien Luce (1858–1941); outside France it was especially effective in Belgium, where through Theo van Rysselberghe (1862–1926) and Henry van de Velde (1863–1957) it not only created a new group, 'The Society of Twenty', but also contributed a great deal of stamina and inspiration to the rather eclectic manifestations of Art Nouveau. In Italy too, where Impressionism itself had had little effect, it was enthusiastically received, though given a literary and naturalistic colouring, in the works of Giovanni Segantini (1859–99) and Gaetano Previati (1852–1920), who transmitted its attitudes to the Futurists.

Neo-Impressionism is clearly the ancestor of most subsequent hard-edge art from Braque to Stella, and in this sense it represents one of the dominant voices in the dialogue of painting. But the other, the 'soft', also stemmed from Impressionism. The importance of creative sincerity, the ability to express emotional reactions freely, to surrender to the instinct of the hand, and a realization of the emotive as well as the descriptive and analytical use of colour – all these are qualities which led through Van Gogh, on whom the works of the Impressionists had a liberating and crucial effect, to the Fauves and on to the Abstract Expressionists.

Far left:

Georges Seurat
Seated Nude: Study for 'Bathing at Asnières' 1883–88

Left:

Georges Seurat
Bridge at Courbevoie 1886–87 (detail)

Right:

Vincent van Gogh
Dr Gachet's Garden, Auvers 1890

2 Symbolism and Art Nouveau

ALASTAIR MACKINTOSH

'There is some fascination to be derived from watching a change in artistic taste, or at any rate an artistic revival, taking place – so to speak – under one's very eyes. Hidden qualities are discovered in pictures hitherto despised or ignored; commercial pressures are applied by the dealers, and speculative buying begins "as in investment"; a cult that was once "camp" soon seems to be merely eccentric and then rather dashing; scholarly articles are written because there is nothing new to be said about established favourites; colour supplements spread the good news to a wider public. From some combination of these and other factors a new taste develops.' (Francis Haskell in *New York Review of Books*, July 1969).

In the passage quoted above Mr Haskell, one of the best historians of artistic taste we have, was discussing French academic painting, but the point that he makes applies to an even greater extent to the subjects of this chapter. In the 1960s an inexpensive book directed at the broad mass of art lovers might have been written about Cubism, Surrealism or Impressionism, but never Symbolism or Art Nouveau. The last-named was considered to be the over-aesthetic last gasp of Victorian vulgarity, while Symbolism was not even well enough known to be dismissed. Clearly a huge shift of taste took place which allowed this chapter to be written.

It can easily be forgotten by the person who is interested in art, visits exhibitions and reads books on the subject that the history of art is not absolute but fluid. Although there are independent-minded people who make their own expeditions into the past, most take their lead from the historians who write the books and organize the exhibitions. The public may influence them by showing a preference for a certain type of art, in this case for a decorative and sensual one, but it will be the historians and the dealers who decide where the next revival is coming from.

Because historians very naturally want to make a name for themselves by rediscovering a new period, and dealers are interested in selling as many works as possible, a revival will usually lead to high claims being made for the art revived. This is certainly true of Symbolism; from being a forgotten or ridiculed style it has swiftly risen to being 'an alternative tradition of modern art', as Alan Bowness put it in the catalogue of the large exhibition which finally accorded Symbolism the accolade of historical respectability: 'French Symbolist Painters' at the Hayward Gallery, London, in 1972. Other writers, such as Phillipe Jullian, go even further and place the Symbolists above the established masters of the birth of modernism.

Odilon Redon
Orpheus c. 1913–16

painter's presence. He enjoyed the cut and thrust of argument and was always open to new ideas. It was this urge to test his theories against other painters whom he admired that led him to Vincent van Gogh, with ultimately tragic results. It is an indication of the accuracy of Gauguin's eye that he, almost alone, understood the value of what Van Gogh was doing.

The two wrote to each other frequently, Gauguin expounding his theories with relish and exuberance and Van Gogh painfully trying to explain his more personal methods. He was aware that he might be susceptible to Gauguin's more powerful personality, and on one occasion let himself be persuaded to paint a picture from his imagination rather than from life. It was the nearest Van Gogh got to Symbolism, and he quickly rejected it. Although the Dutch painter's work has in common the use of 'real' landscape distorted to reflect the emotions of the painter, it lacked the other essential ingredient of Symbolism: the existence of an independent Idea. Van Gogh's paintings are always direct descriptions, while Gauguin's employ the idea of symbolic reference to something other than the ostensible subject.

This can be seen in the portrait Gauguin painted of himself, to send to Van Gogh, which is inscribed *Les Misérables*, a reference to Victor Hugo's novel of an alienated man pursued relentlessly by society. Gauguin's attitude to painting and to himself as a painter is revealed in a letter written to Bernard describing the work: 'I believe it is one of my best efforts, so abstract as to be totally incomprehensible. . . . First the head of a brigand, a Jean Valjean [the hero of *Les Misérables*], personifying a disreputable Impressionist painter likewise burdened forever with the chains of the world. The drawing is altogether peculiar, being complete abstraction. The eyes, the mouth, the nose are like flowers on a Persian carpet, thus personifying the symbolic side. The colour is remote from nature, imagine a confused collection of pottery all twisted by the furnace! All the reds and violets streaked by flames, like a furnace burning fiercely, radiating from the eyes, the seat of the painter's mental struggles. The whole on a chrome background sprinkled with childish nosegays. Chamber of a pure young girl. The Impressionist is such a one, not yet sullied by the filthy kiss of the Académie des Beaux-Arts.'

Gauguin referred to himself as an Impressionist because, although he was reacting against Impressionism, there was still no word to describe his style. None of the Impressionists themselves would have accepted such a romantic and alienated description of the painter's role. The description is also illuminating in showing how Gauguin thought about symbols. Colours and visual emblems are used for their associative value rather than as direct reference. Not many of us nowadays would associate the background wallpaper with the 'chamber of a pure young girl', but we would accept that it does have a certain innocence about it. Gauguin was wise enough not to ram the symbols down our throats by making them too specific, and it is this psychological subtlety that raises him above most other practitioners of Symbolism.

As one might expect, a man of such force of personality and novelty of thought had a considerable effect on those painters who were drawn to him. These included Bernard, Maurice Denis, Paul Sérusier and Charles

Filiger, all of whom passed through a 'Breton' period. Denis and Bernard were attracted by the simple way of life in Brittany, and, using it as subject matter, managed to simplify their own paintings. They took as their method Gauguin's use of flat colour, and at times seem to venture further into the area of decorative abstraction than their master. But neither painter managed to incorporate the philosophical content that was the basis of much of Gauguin's art. Where he succeeded in capturing some of the intensity of the religious feeling native to that part of France, they could only show the colourful patterns of Breton life.

Filiger, on the other hand, was more successful in portraying the piety of the peasants. Intensely religious himself, suffering from guilt about his homosexuality, he found it far easier than his more sophisticated friends. But where they lacked Gauguin's psychological insight, Filiger lacked his aesthetic boldness. Rather than invent a new method of painting, Filiger

Maurice Denis
Breton Dance 1891

Charles Filiger
Breton Cow-herd

Paul Sérusier
Landscape: the Bois d'Amour (The Talisman)
1888

preferred to refurbish the old ones. In this he bears some similarity to the Pre-Raphaelites, in that he also returned to pre-Renaissance sources for inspiration, in his case to Giotto and the Sienese.

Gauguin's most direct disciple was Paul Sérusier, who was a theorist and writer as well as a painter. Sérusier's career shows that he was highly susceptible to influences and picked up theories like blotting paper. His writings are thus more important than his paintings, with one odd exception. This is a work called *The Talisman*, painted on a cigar-box and glowing with rich colour. It was executed in curious circumstances, with Gauguin standing literally at the painter's right hand telling him what to do. 'What colour is that tree?' Gauguin would ask. 'Yellow,' replied Sérusier. 'Then put down yellow.' So Sérusier would apply yellow straight from the tube. The result of this practical lesson he took back with him to Paris and showed all his friends, slightly uncertain whether he was showing them a work by himself or Gauguin. There seems to be no doubt that Sérusier actually painted the picture, but as he never again achieved anything near its quality, the credit for the work should really go to Gauguin, and is another indication of the extraordinary power of the man.

With Gauguin's departure, his followers, as one might expect, were left in disarray. Some stayed on in Brittany, and were forgotten, others returned to Paris to find other umbrellas to shelter under, the Nabi movement being the principal of these. This was a theoretically high-minded ('Nabi' means prophet in Hebrew) but loose grouping of artists including Maurice Denis, Sérusier, Pierre Bonnard, Edouard Vuillard and Paul Ranson, and as one might expect of such an aesthetically diverse body, never produced a style unique to itself. The carefully observed bourgeois interiors of Vuillard have little to do with paintings such as *April* by Maurice Denis.

April is an interesting work because it shows how a painter like Denis, whose sympathies, where subject matter was concerned, were with the main body of the Symbolists but who had learned too much from Gauguin to use their methods, embarked on a path that led towards Art Nouveau. The strongest part of the painting is the organization of the various arabesques that curve across the surface, from the path to the vegetation in the foreground. Denis has attempted to counter this fluidity

Maurice Denis
April 1892

Lucien Lévy-Dhurmer
Our Lady of Penmarc'h 1896

Eugène Grasset
Spring 1884

with a straight fence drawn half way up the painting, but the effect is awkward. The emotional content of the work is no more than a suggestion of mood. The next generation followed illustrators and designers such as Eugène Grasset in retaining the decorative flow of line while rejecting the Symbolist content.

Before we finally leave Brittany for the more civilized decadence of Paris, one curious work demands attention. This is *Our Lady of Penmarc'h* by Lévy-Dhurmer, an artist who painted in various Symbolist styles. The almost *faux-naïf* placing of the figures, and the disturbing degree of realism he brings to the faces, make it a work that could have been painted at any time in the last hundred years, and yet is quite unlike

anything else. That a minor painter can produce one work of such
startling freshness of vision is perhaps indicative of the character of
Symbolism; like its successor, Surrealism, it created the sort of cultural
climate where such flowers could be encouraged to bloom. The same
cannot be said for any of the more systematic approaches to art. Lévy-
Dhurmer was able to experiment in many different Symbolist styles,
bringing to each an eclectic professionalism. His decorative panels of
marsh-birds show a quite different approach to paint from the Breton
picture, the shimmering veils of colour reminding one of Whistler or even
late Monet. If Wagner was the principal musical inspiration of
Symbolism, this work corresponds to Scriabin's chromatic landscapes.

Meanwhile Gauguin himself was pursuing his quest for the primitive to
its logical conclusion. In 1891, just as his stylistic innovations were
beginning to be absorbed and imitated on a wider scale, he left France for
the South Seas. He had understood the central problem of Symbolism,
which was that it was impossible to infuse a painting with mystery and
archetypal meaning if you are carrying around in your luggage the
traditions of French nineteenth-century painting, or, as a later poet put
it, 'You cannot light a match on a crumbling wall,' and in spite of the
time he had spent in Brittany he still felt hemmed in by civilization.

When he finally reached Tahiti, Gauguin found that Western colonial
civilization had already destroyed most of the old culture of the islands,
and that the ease of living he had anticipated was not to be found. It was
only the role he had taken upon himself that kept him going and enabled
him to paint the paradise which he had expected to find, and which, as
he now realized, existed only in his imagination.

His method of painting remained essentially the same as it had been in
Brittany. The painting *Manao Tupapau* is typical of the period. The title
means 'Thinking of the Spirit of the Dead', and it shows a ghostly figure

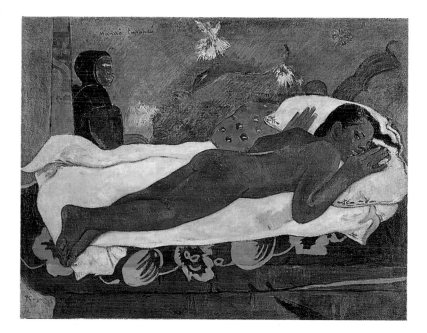

Paul Gauguin
Spirit of the Dead Watching (Manao Tupapau)
1892

During the period of his absence from the Salon, Moreau concentrated on watercolours and oil sketches. Like Gauguin, he realized the necessity for a new visual language, and in many ways his solution was even more startling than Gauguin's and still remains controversial today. Instead of a flat and systematic use of colour for composition, Moreau began to investigate the paint surface itself. He was a great admirer of Baudelaire and Mallarmé, and wished to find a method of painting equivalent to their rich and evocative use of metaphor. His painting style became looser, the pigment being laid on thickly and allowed to create accidents of colour. One could say with some justification that Moreau discovered the principles of Abstract Expressionism, and that by the end of his life he was painting what he called 'colour studies' that rival the best works by Willem De Kooning and Franz Kline, albeit on a far smaller scale.

When he returned to showing his work in public, the change was obvious. Where before the paint had been smooth and the details impeccably painted, now the surface was thick and crusted with colour, brushmarks clearly visible. The paintings caused a sensation, but surprisingly were not vilified like those of the Impressionists, whose style was often more restrained. The public could see that Moreau's work was still Art by its subject matter: *Jacob Wrestling with the Angel*, *David Meditating*, and, endlessly, *Salome*. Salome had become, both for Moreau and for writers such as Mallarmé and Huysmans, the central symbol of the age. Evil and innocent at the same time, exotic and sensual, alluring but dangerous, she exemplified the Symbolist view of women, a view which had become a literary cliché in Romantic poetry. Moreau returned to the subject again and again, showing her dancing before Herod almost naked in a dimly lit temple.

In 1886 Huysmans used Moreau's paintings of Salome to set the scene for his novel *A Rebours*. His hero, a tedious aesthete named Des Esseintes, surrounds himself with 'evocative works of art which would transport him to some unfamiliar world, point out the way to new possibilities and shake up his nervous system by means of erudite fancies, complicated nightmares and suave and sinister visions'. Pride of place in his collection of works by Moreau, Redon and Rodolphe Bresdin goes to Moreau's *Salome*. Huysmans devotes considerable space to a description of this work, and the following should give a flavour of his style:

'With a withdrawn, solemn, almost august expression on her face she begins the lascivious dance which is to rouse the aged Herod's dormant senses; her breasts rise and fall, the nipples hardening at the touch of her whirling necklaces, the strings of diamonds glitter against her moist flesh; her bracelets, her belts, her rings all spit out fiery sparks; and across her triumphal robe, sewn with pearls and patterned with silver, spangled with gold, the jewelled cuirass of which every chain is a precious stone, seems to be ablaze with little snakes of fire, swarming over the matt flesh, over the tea-rose skin, like gorgeous insects with dazzling shards, mottled with carmine, spotted with pale yellow, speckled with steel blue, striped with peacock green.'

This passage, and the use to which Huysmans puts such paintings in his book, gives an idea of the essentially literary interpretation of art common in Symbolist circles. Although Huysmans captures some of the richness of the painting, he adds too many of this own theories and prejudices to be an accurate critic, and his discovery of erotic nightmares in the *Salome* seems to me ridiculous. Moreau's paintings, however much they may try to locate the subconscious levels of myth – and it is doubtful if the painter thought that way at all – remain essentially charming and innocent. His figures evoke characters from a medieval romance rather than chimaeras from the realms of sleep, and the all-over use of colour in continuous arabesques piled one on top of each other implies a positive energy-filled world rather than the negative and decadent end of a culture that Huysmans describes.

Moreau's work remains paradoxical, and in the final analysis, compared to artists such as Gauguin, unsatisfactory. The figures of nubile young girls Moreau was so fond of never quite fit into the almost abstract

Gustave Moreau
Hercules and the Hydra of Lerna c. 1870

Gustave Moreau
Salome Dancing before Herod (Tattooed Salome) 1876 (detail)

formula. In the case of artists discussed so far one feels that the visual is inseparable from the aesthetic issues; while with most Symbolists one feels that the idea came first and the vision followed. The most notorious of Symbolist groups, the Salon de la Rose + Croix, took as their bible the works of Edgar Allan Poe. Poe said of poetry: 'Its sole arbiter is Taste. With the Intellect or with the Conscience, it has only collateral relations. Unless incidentally, it has no concern whatever either with Duty or with Truth.' When Poe refers to Taste he does not necessarily mean the word in terms of good or bad taste: the meaning is that a work of art should be judged by its aesthetic qualities (including its power to stimulate the imagination) rather than its moral content. The French Symbolists were much drawn to Poe's own subject matter, with its haunted castles and necrophiliac heroes; and, like Poe, they often showed woman as beautiful but corrupt, an immaculate and pure skin enclosing a fetid swamp.

To Poe were added Wagner, with his technique of building up passages of augmented triads until the nerves are at breaking point, Baudelaire, Mallarmé and Verlaine, who had begun to investigate these areas in poetry. In painting they drew largely on the academic styles, although artists such as Arnold Böcklin influenced their choice of subject matter. Böcklin's allegories of life and death were immensely popular, and there was a time when an engraving of his *Isle of the Dead* was as *de rigueur* in a fashionable house as a Hockney would be today. His subdued tonality and the classical quality of his figures were a little insipid for the painters of the Rose + Croix, who were aiming at headier brews, but there is little doubt that Böcklin prepared a good deal of the way.

Arnold Böcklin
Isle of the Dead 1886

The English Pre-Raphaelites also had their effect. We shall return to them later; at the moment it is sufficient to point out the similarity between the religious ecstasies depicted by Rossetti and the almost orgasmic self-absorption of many figures in French Symbolist painting. On both sides of the Channel artists were trying to find methods of showing ideas rather than actual events.

Typical of the most extreme elements of the Rose + Croix is the work of Jean Delville, whose paintings usually have a strong Satanic element. Delville had a phenomenal drawing technique and an imagination quite devoid of the usual restraints that an artist imposes on himself. His work often approaches the erotic with a determination that even the most liberated painters of today might balk at. A drawing, *The Idol of Perversity*, of an almost naked figure seen from about the height of the groin, is idealized in that the breasts have a tautness and fullness unobservable in reality and the lips are unbelievably full; it is a fantasy, and its modern equivalent in terms of style is Vargas, the American pin-up artist, although his creations are far cosier.

Satan's Treasures, a large oil painting, also shows Delville's skill in achieving a visual effect. The precision of the drawing is combined with a red so strong that it creates a vibration across the centre of the painting; it is like looking into a fire and half-seeing figures writhing inside it. The arabesque of Satan's wings, if that is what they are, is an effect as

Jean Delville
The Idol of Perversity 1891

Jean Delville
Satan's Treasures 1895

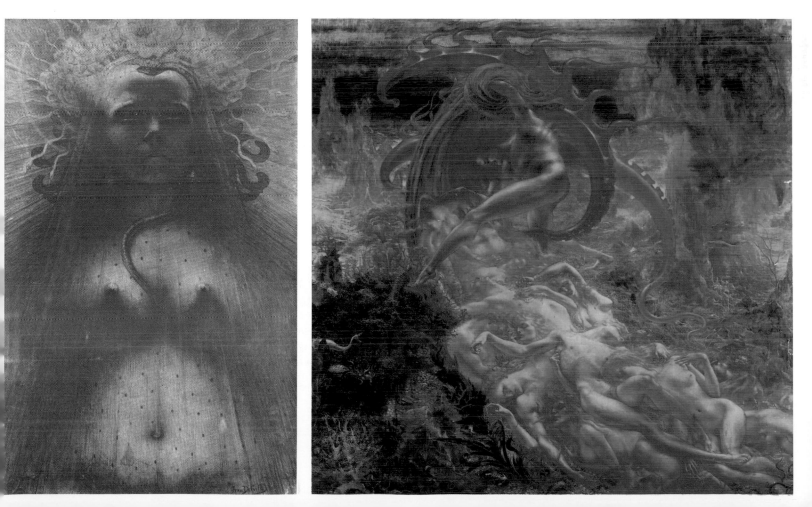

overstated as the quality of the red, and sweeps the eye into a disturbing vortex. It is impossible to look at the work without in some way being affected by it.

Writers on nineteenth-century art differ wildly in their opinions on the quality of paintings such as this. It is obvious that in terms of the central development of art over the last hundred years, this type of Symbolism is quite unrelated to the standards we normally use to judge art. We cannot say it is 'bad', as we might say that André Derain's later work was 'bad' compared to his earlier work, because the intentions of Symbolism are so different from those of the mainstream of modern art. Delville was not interested in making points about the objective nature of art; he wanted to arouse a strong reaction in the viewer. Our own reactions will, of course, be very different from those of the public of the 1890s, for we bring to the paintings an awareness and enjoyment of the discrepancy between intention and effect, which makes it even more difficult to make up our minds.

Many paintings of French Symbolism strike us as absurd, or at least incongruous. Both Point's *The Siren* and Séon's *The Chimaera's Despair* combine a sophisticated approach to colour and brushwork with a ridiculous central figure. In itself, Séon's painting is skilfully composed, with the strong vertical of the cliff giving a curiously unstable effect to the painting, while the cold colours create an intense emotional landscape. Unfortunately the figure of the Chimaera presents more difficult problems which Séon could not resolve. Poets of the time repeatedly referred to Chimaeras, but they could allow the unsettling poetry of the word itself to carry their medium. But the painter has to show what the poet has only to describe, and this desire to follow the poets into essentially literary fields was the undoing of many a Symbolist masterpiece. Séon's Chimaera seems to have strayed out of a literary tea party, and looks more as if she is complaining about the cucumber sandwiches than singing a universal song of archetypal despair.

But Symbolism was nothing if not ambitious, and the artists of the movement were continuously looking for that one stunning image, a metaphor that would illuminate the human condition. Léon Frédéric's *The Lake – The Sleeping Water* comes very close to bringing off an unlikely effect. At first sight the image seems merely sentimental; but the more it is examined the more disturbing it becomes. The sleeping children are drawn with great accuracy of observation, and the swans really seem to be floating over them. The lack of central focus makes the painting seem specific and general at the same time.

Absolute self-confidence was a necessary aspect of the movement in its more public forms such as the Rose + Croix. The doubt and hesitation one finds so often in the work of really great artists had no place in such a deliberate assault on conventional life in the name of hidden truth. It was an inevitable part of the aesthetic of this area of Symbolism that the paintings should exhibit no trace of the self-searchings that appear in the work of Gauguin or even Moreau. This led to a quality which we might call 'synthetic', in the way that Miss World is a 'synthetic' rather than a real woman. The product must show no evidence of hard work or struggle; it must seem effortless and as if it arrived complete.

Alexandre Séon
The Chimaera's Despair 1890

This aspect of Symbolism is at its clearest in the more religiously inclined painters. Satanism and perversity provided one kind of thrill for painters like Delville, but the sicklier aspects of Roman Catholicism offered images of equal emotional weight with the added benefit conferred on sales by respectable sentimentality. Carlos Schwabe was one artist associated with the Rose + Croix who made this area his speciality. His paintings were executed with meticulous regard to detail, and one can often detect the influence of the English Pre-Raphaelites in the early Renaissance quality of his work. His painting of detail is usually far superior to the over-all ordering of the work, as can be seen in the *Virgin of the Lilies*, where the lilies are beautifully observed and then used in a compositional device that looks more like a celestial escalator than anything else. The literalness of the image destroys it. The same can be said of his *Death and the Gravedigger*. The painting very nearly comes off;

Armand Point
The Siren 1897

Léon Frédéric
The Lake – Sleeping Water 1897–98

Medardo Rosso
Infant Laughing 1890

Symbolism in his more erotic works. The way the figures emerge from the 'background' of stone until they are precisely articulated reminds one of Moreau's or even Delville's figures. The smooth perfection of the skin of Rodin's nudes is the opposite of 'realistic' description, and the long curving lines of the bodies are reminiscent of Debussy or Verlaine. There is also a case for considering the Italian sculptor Medardo Rosso as a Symbolist. His works are often made of wax which seems to be melting in front of us. The route that led Rosso to this technique is surely the same as that which led Moreau to his disintegrating paint surface, with the same implication of a world of continuous flux.

In Italy the Symbolist style was softened and used for decorative purposes. The work of Segantini does not strive for the *coup de théâtre* as does so much French Symbolism; he still used the languid ladies so common in art of the period, but we are not asked to believe in them or to take them particularly seriously. The emphasis on the flowing line looks forward to Art Nouveau and is not so far in feeling from the work of the Swiss artist Augusto Giacometti. Both are using the draped female form in essentially decorative work; Giacometti's painting uses the flat areas of colour typical of Art Nouveau, while Segantini is still modelling form in space.

Symbolism, as it has been so far discussed, was very much a Continental phenomenon. Exoticism as a way of life never took root in Britain. When Symbolist ideas crossed the Channel they were pruned of

Giovanni Segantini
The Love Goddess 1894–97

dealing with the physical facts of life in their art, which perhaps explains the delicate awkwardness found in so much of Rossetti.

Burne-Jones, on the other hand, although he too had his vision, was a more earthbound character who had to work hard to bring his painting into line with his imagination. He was also a craftsman, in a sense that Rossetti never claimed to be, and took great delight in experimenting with media such as stained glass, pottery, and book illustration. This professionalism, coupled with a wide knowledge of the history of art, made it difficult for him to find his own voice.

Like the French Symbolists, Burne-Jones turned to myth for his subject matter, but unlike them he was not interested in exotic gods from the east or chimaeras from the murkier aspects of classical myth. His real subject matter took a long time to emerge, but when it did it was a very strange one: sleep. His two masterpieces, the *Briar Rose* series on the legend of the Sleeping Beauty, and *Arthur in Avalon*, both show the principal characters asleep, and many figures from other paintings have the look of somnambulists. Yet these sleeping figures are frequently surrounded by nature in excess and by richly ornamented objects and materials. World-weariness, a favourite theme of the French, had no place in Burne-Jones's scheme; the feeling is rather of imminence – that something will happen rather than that something has happened. The clarity of observation he inherited from the founder members of the Brotherhood, with its resultant three-dimensional depiction of objects and plants, adds to the sense of

Edward Burne-Jones
The Sleeping Beauty 1870–90

beginning and is quite opposite to the sense of dissolution and decay that pervades so much French Symbolism. One has the feeling that the French painters saw themselves as the end of art, the final hectic rhapsody before brute civilization finally takes over, and their works often have an 'end of the world' feeling about them. Burne-Jones's work has none of that sense of doom; perhaps he would have considered it extravagant.

Right:

Edward Burne-Jones
The Golden Stairs 1880

Below:

Edward Burne-Jones
The Beguiling of Merlin 1874

Art Nouveau

The English have never approved of excess, particularly of the gloomy variety; and so it was perhaps inevitable that Art Nouveau, which was partly a reaction against the more portentous elements of Symbolism, should have originated in England with the Arts and Crafts Movement. This was principally inspired by William Morris, who like the other Pre-Raphaelites had been attracted to medieval art. Unlike them, however, he was not content merely to paint pictures influenced by such art; his social concerns led him to a position where he could consider the re-creation of the best aspects of medieval society in the present. One of the fundamental parts of this vision concerned the role of the artist. Morris did not see the artist as an individual standing aloof from society, but as someone emerging naturally from it. He considered that the moment that art lost its decorative and functional basis and became independent of other disciplines, it lost its central purpose of enriching society and became the plaything of rich patrons.

Accordingly Morris concentrated on reviving the idea of applied art. His own speciality was fabric and wallpaper design, but he also acted as a focal point for many other craftsmen and artists. He knew the work of A. H. Mackmurdo and his disciple C. A. Voysey, although neither artist could be said to be directly under his influence.

The achievement of this group of designers was radically to rethink the concept of pattern. Before Morris, fabric design had tended to be three-dimensional and illusionistic in character. Large bunches of cabbage roses would be drawn with some perspective and shading, an effect that tended to be fussy and negate the inescapable two-dimensionality of a floor or a wall. Morris flattened out the design, removing any attempt to show flowers or birds realistically. The emphasis was switched from the subject matter to colour and line of great richness and complexity.

For inspiration Morris looked at any part of the history of art that struck him as useful, to medieval tapestry, to Jacobean hangings and to Oriental design. This eclectic method was picked up by those around him: for instance, William de Morgan, the group's ceramicist, studied Islamic and Hispano–Moresque pottery and as a result rediscovered lustre techniques that had been largely forgotten.

By the 1880s a growing body of connoisseurs was buying the products of the Arts and Crafts Movement. Fashionable houses were entirely papered and hung with Morris designs, and pots by De Morgan and paintings by Burne-Jones would be bought to complete the whole. Even Pre-Raphaelite styles of dress were copied as the idea of living aesthetically caught on. Because the art was applied, it needed to be used to fulfil its role, and this enabled non-artists to take part in the movement. The same process can be seen in the emergence of Pop styles in the mid-1960s.

This way of looking at art as part of the fabric of living meant that artists could apply themselves to a wide choice of media. Where before an artist was someone who painted pictures or made sculpture, now he could design wallpaper, make pottery or illustrate books. This enabled artists such as Aubrey Beardsley to find their true role.

William de Morgan
Twin-handled amphora in Persian colouring, 1888–97

Above, left:

Arthur Mackmurdo
Textile design, 1884

Above, right:

Charles Voysey
Tulip and Bird wallpaper, 1896

William Morris
Daffodil chintz, 1891

formal coherence, inherited from Cézanne, which he was never to
abandon. There was clearly something in the air at the moment which
transcended personal contacts and coteries, for in Barcelona, for instance,
nineteen-year-old Pablo Picasso was painting pictures such as *The Window*
which showed the same tendency for forms to dissolve in, and be moulded
by, evocative colour; in Picasso's case they were less pure, less
adventurous, echoing the palette of Manet rather than venturing into
new chromatic dimensions.

   Personal contacts, however, were the flashpoint which ignited Fauvism.
The common experiences of Moreau's studio were extended in 1899 at
the Académie Carrière, where Matisse met two painters from the Paris
suburb of Chatou, André Derain and the self-taught Maurice de
Vlaminck, both of whom were making adventurous visual experiments in

Pablo Picasso
The Window 1900

Maurice de Vlaminck
The Bar Counter 1900

Henri Matisse
Nude in the Studio 1898

the same direction under the influence of Van Gogh. Vlaminck, an explosive, naturally gifted, physically vital man, an anarchist and a champion cyclist, who once said that he loved Van Gogh more than his own father, obviously owed something to his Flemish ancestry. Consumed with a passion for brutal truth, he crucified his sitters with something approaching relish, handling paint with a Chardin-like verve.

Matisse was to build his subsequent career on his experiences and discoveries during this period, in which he produced some of his most spectacular works. The continuing evolution of colour and its emancipation from accepted perceptual conventions led to an increasing concern with what he called 'pictorial mechanism', which owed a lot to the disciplines of Seurat's Pointillism: its structural purity and use of dots of pure colour. Abandoning realism, he kept a tangential hold on reality;

and even in a painting such as *Luxury I* he not only retained spatial depth, but arranged the figures in a composition which would not have been unfamiliar to an artist of the Renaissance. They are simplified, stylized, but not distorted for any emotive reason. At the same time, however, they convey perfectly the resonances of the title.

Among Matisse's associates in the early 1900s, the closest to him was Albert Marquet. From a style close to the bold formalism of Edouard Vuillard and the other members of the Nabi group of the 1890s, Marquet migrated to one which, though expressive in form and technique, eschewed the pure brilliant colours of Vlaminck or Matisse, and kept much closer to figurative sources. In *Matisse Painting a Nude*, for instance, the colour appears rather as a background than as an integral part of the whole composition; the figure is defined by a line, and not modelled by the surrounding areas of colour. There is also apparent Marquet's growing concern with a subdued palette, and with the potentialities of a luminous black; in many ways he reverted to a Manet-like approach to painting, and his draughtmanship was such that Matisse once described him, with some pertinence, as 'the French Hokusai'.

André Derain brought to the Fauves something of the same vigour and panache as his friend Vlaminck; he too used colour directly from the tube, applied in broken lines with quick impetuous brush-strokes; but

Henri Matisse
The Green Stripe 1905

Henri Matisse
Luxury I 1907

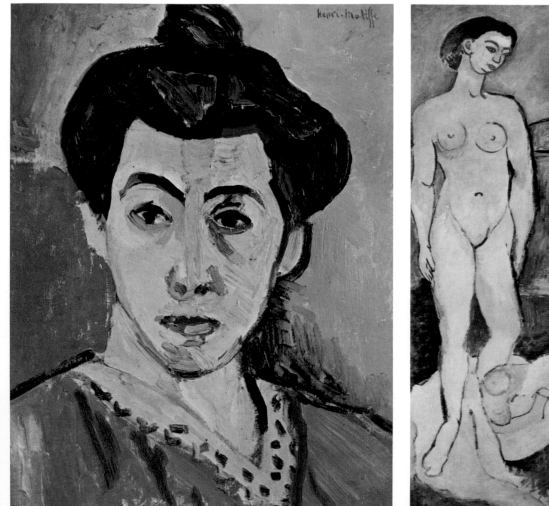

Albert Marquet
*Matisse Painting a Nude in Henri Manguin's
Studio* 1904–05

even in his youthful works he was more lucid, more thoughtful, more graceful. Conscious of the past, his discovery of the emotive use of colour owed as much to the Pointillists as it did to Van Gogh, and his forms were influenced by a variety of precedents: *Images d'Epinal*, those simple folk-images which had so appealed to Courbet and Gauguin; Byzantine art; and the simplified planes of African sculpture. In 1905, the year in which he visited London and painted scenes on the Thames, he produced views of the Seine in which Seurat's Pointillist technique is allied to Van Gogh's hatched brush-strokes to produce works of organized lucidity, remarkable for their emotional coherence.

Face to face with a living model, however, Derain's work took on greater immediacy; and in *Lady in a Chemise* he came close to the impetuous vehemence which was at the heart of Fauvism. The multiplicity of colours and tones, the flickering flame-like brushwork, the exaggeration of the face and eyes, the heavily pendulous and slightly distorted left hand, the partial use of a contour line to define those parts of the figure which play a dominant part in the composition, create an impression of adventurousness which in the long run turned out to be alien to his talent.

'How, with what I have here, can I succeed in rendering, not what I see, but what is, what has an existence for me, *my reality*, then set to work drawing, taking from nature what suits my needs? I drew the contours of each object in black mixed with white, each time leaving in the middle of the paper a blank space which I then coloured in with a specific and quite intense tone. What did I have? Blue, green, ochre, not many colours. But the result surprised me. I had discovered what I was really looking for.' The description which Raoul Dufy gave, many years later, of his conversion to the ideas of Fauvism, describes as well as anything the sense of elated emancipation which so many of his contemporaries felt, and it is immediately apparent in his paintings of this period; they have a chunky vitality which his later, more graceful and sophisticated works

André Derain
Banks of the Seine at Pecq 1905 (detail)

André Derain
Lady in a Chemise 1906

Raoul Dufy
Placards at Trouville 1906

Othon Friesz
Sunday at Honfleur 1907

were to lose completely. *Placards at Trouville*, with its movement, its bold simplified outlines, its areas of bright colour, each emitting an air of joyous sensationalism, conveys perfectly the sense of seaside holiday-making in fresh sparkling air. Born at Le Havre, Othon Friesz studied at school under the same teachers as Dufy, and he too was fascinated by seaside subjects. His *Sunday at Honfleur*, painted a year after Dufy's exercise at Trouville, emphasizes the differences between them. The composition is more static, the colour less adventurous, the lines heavier, more dominant; the desire to charge the canvas with some kind of lyrical emotion is more apparent, and therefore less successful. Friesz's thirst for visual eloquence was to lead him eventually to a baroque exuberance which verged on the hysterical.

The Fauve experience was for many artists a period of liberation, marking the moment at which they escaped from the conventions of realism and the confines of the conventional palette to achieve a realization, on which their future careers would be built, that the artist was concerned with the primacy of his own personal vision, and with creating a world which he himself controlled. This is especially evident in the case of Georges Braque, who was, like Friesz, a native of Le Havre. It was Friesz who first introduced him to what the Fauves were doing; and for some three years, between 1904 and 1907, he produced a series of works which, though vivid in colour and exuberant in line, are thoughtful in composition, velvety in texture, and more deliberate in execution than the general run of paintings his friends were producing. Already there was implicit in them a concern with construction, a tendency to flatness of composition, which foreshadowed the emergence of Cubism. But artists such as Robert Delaunay, who themselves were never Fauves, and who went on to Cubism, Futurism or any of the other subsequent movements which the Fauve revolt had made possible, always retained strong evidence of its influence in their works, paying unconscious tribute to its liberating force, and to the new significance which it had given to colour.

This was even more true of those artists whom one might define as unconscious Fauves, of whom the most outstanding example was Georges Rouault. A pupil of Moreau, and at one time marginally connected with Matisse's group, Rouault never really felt in sympathy with the movement, although he was equally concerned with wringing anguish from his colours, and using art as a means of expressing a personal, anti-realist viewpoint. The two dominant elements in his creative make-up were his early experiences as an apprentice to a maker of stained glass, and his friendship with two prominent figures in the Catholic revival which had such an important influence in the cultural life of the early twentieth century: J. K. Huysmans, a convert who united the fervours of belief with the recently shed languors of decadence, and Léon Bloy, one of the new school of writers who combined a radical

Georges Rouault
Bal Tabarin (Dancing the Chahut) 1905

Georges Rouault
Versailles: the Fountain 1905

concern about social justice with an almost excessive passion for the traditional values which he saw enshrined in Christianity. From these combined sources Rouault built up a style which varied little throughout the whole of his career. From his religious and social preoccupations he evolved an iconography which dealt with religious subjects, with whores and clowns, with all that involved the grandeurs and miseries of *la condition humaine*, and a passion tinged with bitter irony, even pessimism. From his feeling for the translucent beauty of stained glass he evolved a style characterized by its craftsmanship, its Byzantine simplicity, its luminous colours. But, in spite of these personal manncrisms, Rouault was still at heart a Fauve. The sense of stylistic passion, the savage slashes of colour, the need for vehemence, become more apparent when, as in *Versailles: The Fountain*, the subject matter is not overtly Expressionistic.

Kees van Dongen
The Speech 1904–05

The extent of Rouault's Fauvism can be assessed by comparing his work with that of the happy, extroverted Kees van Dongen, an instinctive, archetypal Bohemian, who also had a penchant for painting clowns and the demi-monde, and whose finest work has an exuberant panache, an evocative passion, which seduce rather than convince. His momentary strengths and his eventual weaknesses sprang from the fact that he was a natural painter. A member of the Fauves, he later went on to join the German group Die Brücke (*see* p. 132), and in this context demonstrated the gulf which existed between those artists to whom passion in painting was a matter of style and those for whom it was a way of life.

A Northern Episode

The almost irresistible urge to identify the genius of Expressionism with that of Nordic cultures – and to relate its degrees of intensity to the distance which separated its practitioners from the shores of the Mediterranean and the influences of Catholicism – receives its most cogent support from the work and personality of Edvard Munch, whose paintings have become the very archetypes of all that the movement implied. A Norwegian, he was nourished in the same traditions which produced the guilt-tinged work of Ibsen and Strindberg (who wrote a catalogue entry to his *The Kiss*). Profoundly neurotic, his childhood was spent in the most inauspicious circumstances: his mother died when he was five, and one of his sisters when he was thirteen; his father was a doctor who practised in a poverty-ridden area of Löiten. He grew up in an atmosphere dominated by the ideas of death, disease and anxiety, and the images of this period of his life were always to remain with him. In the *Madonna* of 1895–1902, for instance, the typically 'decadent' concept of the subject as a nearly nude, whore-like figure is reinforced by a painted border of spermatozoa, which lead to an embryo in the lower left-hand corner, derived from an illustration in a German anatomical text-book published in the middle of the century, and presumably forming part of his father's library.

Significantly enough, Aubrey Beardsley made use of the identical figure in several of his drawings; which underlines the fact that many artists who came to creative maturity in the later nineteenth century were obsessed with the same symbols, the same preoccupations. The concept of the *femme fatale*, using the phrase in its literal sense, to indicate the idea of woman as a malevolent, destructive and seductive siren, played a vital part in the work of Munch. Time and time again he reverts to the theme of woman as vampire, as the fatal temptress, and even in his *Madonnas* he seems intent on destroying utterly the icon which in the past had done so much to idealize femininity.

No less was he seduced by the idea of death and disease. In part this may have been due to the circumstances of his childhood; death struggles, sick rooms and the paraphernalia of mortality intrigued him as much as the themes of classical mythology had obsessed Poussin. But there was more to it than that. The idea of eventual personal annihilation has always been emotive, and the nineteenth century was more than half in love with

Edvard Munch
Madonna 1895–1902

Edvard Munch
Death and the Maiden 1893

easeful death. Queen Victoria was as susceptible to the idea as Munch, and in some curious way – partly at least explained by Mario Praz – it had become intermingled with sexuality. Keats, Schubert, Schiller and many others had underlined the connection in the early part of the century; the Belgian Antoine Wiertz (1806–65) devoted his whole artistic career to the theme, and bequeathed to an ungrateful posterity a museum commemorating the fact. But nowhere – because he bent his technique to underlining his image – has the idea been better elaborated than in Munch's *Death and the Maiden* of 1893. On the left of the picture wriggle the spermatozoic shapes; on the right is a frieze composed of two foetus-like creatures. Death himself is no traditional Gothic-horror skeleton, though the black branch-like lines which echo his shape suggest the anatomical: he is a semi-human shape, full of amorphous ambiguities, the sense of horror emphasized by the wooden leg-stump which emerges through the girl's thigh. She, on the other hand, is characterized by an exuberant sensuality, underlined in a formal sense by the heaviness of her thighs, the solidity of her buttocks, the bluntness of her face, and the exaggeration of the line which runs from her left armpit to her knee.

That Munch had personality problems more pressing than those which beset the generality of mankind is obvious, and it would be ridiculous to disregard them in assessing the nature of his work. His neuroses are apparent in such a way that the work is often the graphic expression of actual experience. He was conscious of this, and in his diary he records the experience which created one of his most symptomatic subjects, *The Scream*. 'I was walking along the road with two friends. The sun was setting, and I began to be afflicted with a sense of melancholy. Suddenly the sky became blood-red. I stopped and leaned against a fence, feeling dead-tired, and stared at the flaming clouds that hung, like blood and a sword, over the blue-black fjord and the city. My friends walked on. I stood riveted, trembling with fright. And I heard (felt) a loud, unending scream piercing nature.'

The experience, then, although psychological in origin, was as real to him as to a mystic. But many have had similar sensations; what was in a sense unique about Munch was that within the traditional framework of the European artistic tradition, he forged a remarkably expressive – the adjective is inescapable – visual technique, combining the curved whiplash line of Art Nouveau with colours which range from the acidulous to the sentimental in a frenzy of compositional vigour which is often strongly reminiscent of Van Gogh. Nor is the stylistic affinity accidental. In 1889 Munch had travelled to Paris on a state scholarship and had come into contact with Van Gogh and Gauguin – the latter, as usual with younger artists, exerting a strong influence on him. In 1892 he was invited to exhibit at the Verein der Berliner Künstler, where, after a great deal of controversy which helped to impress Munch on the German artistic awareness, and led to the foundation of the Berlin Secession, the leaders of the society closed the exhibition in which he was participating. But it was in the German capital that he came into fruitful contact with the poet Richard Dehmel, the critic and historian Julius Meier-Graefe, the enlightened industrialist Walter Rathenau (who first bought a Munch painting in 1893) and Strindberg. By 1895 he was back in Paris again, and for the next few years lived a cosmopolitan existence, though forced to spend occasional periods in a sanatorium. In 1908 he suffered a complete collapse and spent a year in Dr Daniel Jacobson's hospital in Copenhagen. In 1909 he returned to Norway and passed the rest of his life there in relative seclusion.

Like his literary compatriots, Munch was preoccupied with feelings rather than objects, and above all else with their effects on people and their relationships. In this latter respect he was unusual among the Expressionists. This is apparent especially in the contrast between his work and that of his Belgian contemporary James Ensor, with whom, in other respects, he has many affinities. Both were ecstatic in their approach; both concerned themselves with the dark underside of life; and yet both drew support and nourishment from the traditional elements of art – though this was more apparent with Ensor, whose affinities with Turner, and even with Chardin, need no underlining. Even physically they were rather alike. But the style is almost invariably the man, and

Edvard Munch
The Scream 1893

Ensor seems through his Flemish mother to have established instinctive
contact with the cultural tradition which she represented. It was derived
not from the Italianate episodes of the seventeenth century as represented
by Rubens, nor from the French-orientated style of the Walloons, but
from a stream of uninhibited visual fantasy, interlaced with bucolic
folklore, which, stretching back to the Middle Ages, had found its
supreme expression in the works of Pieter Bruegel, and which, continuing
into the twentieth century, has helped (largely through Belgian artists
such as Magritte and Delvaux) to link Expressionism with Surrealism.
Ensor marks, more clearly than any other artist the line of continuity
between the so-called 'Nibelungen Expressionists' – Hieronymous Bosch,
Urs Graf, Hans Baldung Grien – and the artists of the late nineteenth and
early twentieth century.

Satirical, compassionate, acerbic and whimsical, Ensor created a
universe of his own, peopled with absurd, tawdry, moving, shocking
figures which grip the imagination, stimulate the fancy and by their very

vehemence produce just that shock to the susceptibilities of the spectator which is the prime goal of Expressionism. *Skeletons Warming Themselves at a Stove* might well be an epitome of the whole movement: the macabre theme, the sinister whimsicality of the scattered skulls grouped grotesquely in a clumsy pyramid around the stove, the minatory figure in the right-hand corner of the composition. But despite the subject matter – and this is a consistent element in Ensor's work – the colouring has a light, sensuous quality, which verges on the lyrical, and underlines his debt to the Impressionists. It was only in his early phase that his technique verged on the sombre, and even then it had a delicate, velvety texture.

   Skeletons Warming Themselves at a Stove looks almost as though it might be an illustration of some pungent, folksy proverb, and though Ensor was capable of painting such pictures as *The Ray* which have no meaning other than that conveyed by the form and colour, there are always literary and social implications in his major works. They are commentaries, even though the precise nature of the moral is never clearly indicated. This is especially true of the *Entry of Christ into Brussels*, which packs into one massive composition (250 × 434 cm) a whole host of satirical, grotesque episodes and situations. A great mass of ugly, distorted faces; Christ mounted on an ass; a broad banner with the inscription *Vive la Sociale*: the whole thing is like some mad *kermesse*

James Ensor
The Singular Masks 1891

James Ensor
Skeletons Warming Themselves at a Stove 1889

portrayed in a manner which hints at a parody of a historical *grande machine* by a Baroque artist. Again, the colours are light, lyrical, but emphatically dissonant; and the substructure of drawing is marked by a deliberate coarseness – vulgarity would not be too strong a word – which underlines one of Ensor's greatest contributions to the vocabulary of Expressionism, the use of line to create an emotive effect independently of colour. It was this quality which especially endeared him to Paul Klee, and to Emil Nolde, both of whom derived a great deal from his influence. It is important to remember that Ensor produced his most significant work in the last twenty years of the nineteenth century – *The Entry of Christ into Brussels* was painted in 1889 – and that, more forcibly than Gauguin, and even than Van Gogh, he assailed the primacy of the representational element in art, deriving his inspiration largely from that one area in which it had never played an important part – caricature. At the same time too his exploration of the incongruous and the irrational anticipated developments which would not become apparent in the mainstream of art until the second decade of the twentieth century. Life, death, the absurd grandeur of the human condition, were themes which obsessed him, whatever the changes which took place in a style which showed at times the influence of Turner, of Constable and of Rowlandson (in the Royal Museum at Antwerp there are copies by him of works by all three of these). An assiduous student of the great printmakers and

James Ensor
The Entry of Christ into Brussels 1889

etchers (Rembrandt, Callot, Daumier and Forain were his favourites), he produced, especially in the 1880s, a great number of etchings and other monochrome works in which Goyaesque fantasy illumines disciplined skill.

He was subject to the ambiguities of his time, and though public recognition came late, he could well be claimed as a precursor by Fauves, Expressionists and Surrealists alike; while, equally, the Symbolists might have observed in his work strong elements of their own preoccupation with metaphysical references. He was, after all, the compatriot and largely the contemporary of Emile Verhaeren and Maurice Maeterlinck. His iconography with its strong allusive qualities would have been acceptable to artists who eschewed the violence of his technique, and his preoccupation with those imaginative resonances which were the concern of painters as disparate as Redon and Klimt is suggested by his concern with masks – as in the famous *Self-portrait with Masks*. The autobiographical source of these (as well as of his concern with shells and Chinese porcelain) was doubtless the stall which his mother used to run on the front at Ostend. But they came to possess for him an abiding significance, reflecting at once the psychic anomalies of his own life and the baffling enigmas of interpersonal relationships. Masked figures were almost a cliché of Symbolist art, but Ensor was the first to raise them to the status of independent entities, suggestive question-marks in the carnival of life.

Although he was a co-founder of the avant-garde group Les XX, which exhibited Seurat's *A Sunday Afternoon at the Island of La Grande Jatte* in 1887, Ensor did not start to receive real recognition until the 1920s, by which time he had long done his best work. But he did play a significant part in forming the considerable tradition of Belgian Expressionism, itself a vital link in the transmission of all that the movement implied to later generations.

The links between Paris and Brussels had always been close, and a typical transitional figure was Rik Wouters, who, commencing as a self-taught artist, visited Paris, where he came under the influence of Degas and Cézanne, to whom, superficially, his style owes a great deal. But in his case what might have been little more than a kind of derivative Post-Impressionism was transformed, partly through the influence of Ensor, partly through the consuming passion which he felt for his wife Nel, into something much more dynamic, broad in handling, lyrically emotive in colouring, with passages of rich vibrancy which suggest the basic grammar of pure Expressionism.

For him there was never any precise moment of conversion; perhaps his life was too short for that, and a more typical figure was Gust de Smet, whose career illuminates the way in which the dormant inclination to Expressionism which was inherent in Flemish art could be triggered off by external stimuli into something closer to our conception of an international style. When in Holland he broke away from the luminist tradition which he had derived from the Impressionists, and, largely through the magazine *Das Kunstblatt*, became familiar with what was happening in Germany. His art became wilder, more tragic, the brushwork quick, nervous, ecstatic, with sombre earthen colours, and he chose for his subjects those emotion-laden themes – prostitutes, circus people, peasants – which had come to be accepted as the accredited icons of twentieth-century romanticism. After flirting for a while with the structural dynamics of Cubism, he reverted in the 1930s to paintings in which the sonorous play of light and colour within a clearly defined outline evokes a sense of passionate sensuality.

If Bruegel was Flemish, so too was Rubens, and the particular brand of Expressionism which dominated Flanders for the first quarter of this century was on the whole humane rather than violent, lyrical rather than vehement; an Expressionism of the brush rather than of the heart. This was as true of De Smet as it was of his friend and contemporary Constant Permeke, who also started off his artistic career in the Impressionist-inclined artists' colony of Sint-Matens-Latem, and then developed an emotive monumentality which retained Ensor's sense of near-abstraction and visual violence. Objects ceased to be clearly visible, and were discernible rather than apparent; there was a largeness of treatment, an air of the cosmic about both his figures and his landscapes. Wounded in the war, Permeke lived for five years in considerable poverty among the farmers of Devonshire, an experience which confirmed in him that penchant for a kind of rural mysticism which was one of the minor

Rik Wouters
Nel Wouters 1912

Gust de Smet
The Striped Skirt 1941

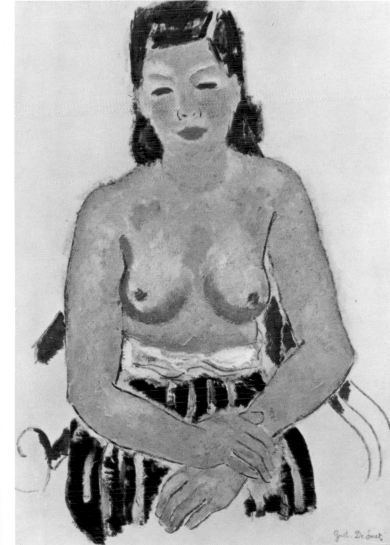

Leon Spilliaert
Tall Trees 1921

strands in the Expressionist tradition, deriving its sanction from both Van Gogh and the Pont Aven school. The sense of lyrical rapture infuses his paintings with a Turneresque quality which may have been consciously acquired in England, but more directly it permits the unification of a whole variety of disparate objects – trees, houses, windmills – which assume a limpid plasticity within an all-embracing light.

Léon Spilliaert, although self-taught, was formally more sophisticated, his art more elusive. Untouched by Ensor, but owing much to Munch, his earliest works have strong Symbolist characteristics, the linear arabesques which dominate them suggesting an impassioned Art Nouveau with emotional undercurrents alien to that more purely decorative style. But from the very beginning, his paintings had an unreal, hallucinatory quality, and certain images obsessed him – girls by the seaside, human beings confronting and being absorbed by nature. Trees came to play an increasingly dominant role in his imagery, and he observed them with a frenzied intensity which converts them from inanimate phenomena into brooding totems, transforming their surroundings into landscapes of the mind heavy with hidden significances. More clearly than any of his contemporaries, he shows the intricacy of the network which linked Symbolism, Expressionism and Surrealism.

Germany: Die Brücke

A good deal of the impetus which Expressionism in Belgium received came from the presence there during the Great War of a number of German artists, most of them working in a medical unit. Erich Heckel, for instance, was stationed in Ostend, came into contact with Ensor, and painted his lost *Ostend Madonna* in 1915 on the canvas of an army tent. This underlines the fact that although Expressionism was a European phenomenon, it was in Germany that it achieved hegemony. It was there that it became almost a way of life, and it was there that it assumed its most radical and influential forms. The reasons for this cannot be restricted to mere stylistic evolution or changing aesthetic credos. Dangerous though it may be to make generalizations about the pattern of national cultures, it seems impossible to evade the realization that of all European peoples, the German-speaking have been the most apt to emphasize feeling, to prefer the world of the imagination to that of fact, to be seduced by the concept of storm and stress, to toy with the ideas of darkness and cruelty. This was no new thing. The sadistic iconography of Grünewald, the violence of popular German art, especially in the field of graphic reproduction; the fact that, for instance, of the seven 'horrid' novels Jane Austen mentions in *Northanger Abbey* two are actual translations from the German, and four others are set in Germany; the popularity of stories such as that of *Struwwelpeter* all point to a continuity of interest in the macabre. John Willett, in his lively history of Expressionism, makes the point that the poet Johannes Becher, a leading figure in literary Expressionism, could quote with approval this passage from the seventeenth-century poet Andreas Gryphius:

Oh the cry!
Murder! Death! Misery! Torments! Cross! Rack!
    Worms! Fear!
Pitch! Torture! Hangman! Flame! Stink! Cold!
    Ghosts! Despair!
O! Pass by!
Deep and high!
Sea! Hills! Mountains! Cliff! Pain no man can bear!
Engulf, engulf, abyss! those endless cries you hear.

It could well be a catalogue of Expressionist iconography.

Reinforced by its self-imposed function as the guardian of the West against the Slavonic hordes, nourished by the horrors of the Thirty Years

War, the German spirit alternated between apocalyptic idealism and intellectual masochism. The patterns of history did little to relieve these tensions. Between its beginnings as a united nation in 1870, and the advent of Hitler some sixty years later, it endured the hysterical imperialism of the Hohenzollerns, the privations of the Great War, the miseries of inflation, the tragedies of the Weimar experiment. Catastrophe or the millennium seemed always to be on the horizons of German experience. The music of Wagner and of Richard Strauss; the writings of Nietzsche and Heinrich Mann; the plays of Strindberg (which were very popular in Germany) and Wedekind, all nourished that sense of revolutionary emotional turbulence which drove the artists of Berlin, Munich, Dresden and Vienna far beyond the limits reached by their more restrained contemporaries west of the Rhine. In Germany, to an extent unknown in any other country, Expressionism dominated painting and sculpture, literature, the theatre and the cinema.

Unlike France, with its strong traditions of unified political history and centralization, Germany still retained that regionalism which the creation of the Empire under Prussian rule had hidden rather than destroyed. Although the first stirring of a new movement in the arts was nourished by the presence in Germany during the 1890s of Munch who had a *succès de scandale* at the exhibition of the Verein der Berliner Künstler (a dominantly Impressionist body) in 1892, and by the steadily widening influence of Gauguin and of Van Gogh, its final realization was regional rather than national.

Die Brücke ('The Bridge'), which has justly been described as commencing more like a revolutionary cell than an art movement, was founded in 1905 by four refugees from the school of architecture at Dresden, the capital of Saxony. They had no experience of painting, but they saw in it a means of liberation, a medium for expressing a social message. In the programme which one of them, Ernst Ludwig Kirchner, composed and engraved on wood for the group in 1906, he wrote:

'Believing as we do in growth, and in a new generation, both of those who create and those who enjoy, we call all young people together, and as young people, who carry the future in us, we want to wrest freedom for our actions and our lives from the older, comfortably established forces. We claim as our own everyone who reproduces directly, and without falsification, whatever it is that drives him to create.' Influenced by Van Gogh, by medieval German woodcuts, and by African and Oceanic sculpture, Kirchner was concerned with exploiting every technical and compositional technique which could convey a sense of immediate vivid sensation, mixing petrol into his oil paints so that they dried quickly with a matt finish, excelling in watercolour, often in conjunction with other media, applying bright local colour with small brush-strokes. His chromatic inventiveness was, within his own context, remarkably revolutionary: he would harmonize reds and blues, black and purple, yellow and ochre, brown and cobalt blue. Indeed all his earlier works show the self-education of an artist untrammelled by formal education.

By 1911, therefore, when he and his friends decided to move to the more metropolitan atmosphere of Berlin, Kirchner had acquired considerable technical skills, designed for his own purpose, but had not

Ernst Kirchner
Programme of *Die Brücke* 1905

yet lost a certain innocence of visual approach. All this is summed up in *Semi-nude Woman with Hat*, painted in that year. Broad and simple in conception, parsimonious almost in its range of colours, it is a simple dynamic composition, depending on the use of contrasting and complementary arcs. One series starts with the top of the hat and is continued through the shoulders and arms. Another commences with the brim of the hat, is half-echoed in the chin, doubled in the breasts, and concludes with the lines of the blouse. As a counterpoint to this theme is another, consisting of triangles; the first in the lower section of the hat where it reveals the woman's forehead, the second, inverted at the throat, is echoed in the armpits and the fingers of her left hand. The broadly brushed-in background serves as a counterfoil to the figure, whose face, while it suggests the influence of primitive sculpture, is also marked by a kind of suggestive eroticism. The Expressionists as a whole were to be enamoured of the Brechtian underworld of Berlin, with its whores, pimps and gangsters who contrasted so strongly with the apparent simple purity of their own dreamworld. How powerful the effect was on Kirchner is especially apparent in works such as *Five Women in the Street*, in which the ominous black figures, with their sinister, elongated bodies and fantastic hats, are sited against a virulent green background, which, though it retains a few elements of figurative observation, is virtually abstract and of considerable compositional complexity. Sculptural influences are again apparent; but the whole painting is massively dedicated to representing the artist's own sense of projected sin, Puritan in intention, passionate in expression. Significantly, five years later, when on the verge of physical and mental collapse, he wrote; 'I stagger to work, but all my work is in

Ernst Kirchner
Figures on Stones (Fehmarn) 1912–13

Ernst Kirchner
Semi-nude Woman with Hat 1911

Ernst Kirchner
Five Women in the Street 1913

vain, and the mediocre tears everything down in its onslaught. I'm now like the whores I used to paint.'

After his breakdown he went to Switzerland, and there found annealing but less emotive themes in the contemplation of landscape, and in the idealization of those peasants of Davos whose staple industry for the last century seems to have been the inspiration of neurasthenic Northerners. Though still showing a certain violent grandeur of conception, his post-war works never really lived up to the earlier works, with their overriding sense of passionate apprehension.

Erich Heckel was in some ways more restrained than the other members of Die Brücke, even though his technique was occasionally more adventurous. His first paintings have the uncontrolled vehemence of the newcomer overwhelmed by the freedom which art gives him, intoxicated by the sense of apparently limitless power which it seems to confer on its practitioners. *Brickworks* of 1907, for instance, has been painted by squeezing oil out of the tubes straight on to the canvas, and using the brush only to tidy up the total effect. Colours and forms swirl together in a kind of pictorial storm. The visual impact – an extremely moving one – has nothing to do with the actual theme; it is created entirely by the medium, which has a life and movement all of its own. The pure, undiluted pigment has the same vehemence as in some of Van Gogh's paintings.

There was something touchingly idealistic – and German – in Heckel's devotion to the concept of the group to which he belonged at this period – reminiscent both of the ideals of the nineteenth-century Romantic religious painters, the Nazarenes, and of the less admirable duelling clubs. It was he who procured their communal studios and organized their first exhibition and their shared holidays on the Moritzburg lakes. In 1909 Heckel travelled extensively in Italy, was impressed by Etruscan art, fascinated by the idea of light, and set out to express in his work those qualities of formal coherence which he had discovered south of the Alps. The first fruit of this new inclination, and possibly his finest painting, is the *Nude on a Sofa*, in which the singing colours and gently hedonistic image are set off by the vigour of the composition and the nervous, ecstatic brushwork. At first glance it is closer to the Fauves than to their German Expressionist contemporaries, but no Frenchman would have been quite so peremptory in his treatment of the feet, nor so emotive in the handling of the walls and window. In a sense, *Nude on a Sofa* exemplifies perfectly Kirchner's clarification of the original Brücke declaration: 'Painting is the art which represents a phenomenon of feeling on a plane surface. The medium employed in painting, for both background and line, is colour. The painter transforms a concept derived from his own experiences into a work of art. He learns to make use of his medium through continuous practice. There are no fixed rules for this. The rules for any given work grow during its actual execution, through the personality of the creator, his methods and technique, and the message he is conveying. The perceptible joy in the object seen is, from the beginning, the origin of all representational art. Today photography

Erich Heckel
Brickworks 1907

Erich Heckel
Nude on a Sofa 1909

reproduces an object exactly. Painting, liberated from the need to do so, regains freedom of action. Instinctive transfiguration of form, at the very instant of feeling, is put down on the flat surface on impulse. The work of art is born from the total translation of personal ideas in the execution.'

In fact, in becoming more surface-orientated, Heckel's work, with its geometricized transcriptions of light and form, its sharp, angular contours and its figurative stylization, became the virtual standard of the Brücke contribution to the art of the twentieth century. It is nevertheless exceptional in possessing strong human sympathies, which have nothing to do with social protest, and an interest in narrative which secured him a considerable degree of popular success long before his fellow members achieved it.

Karl Schmidt-Rottluff, the third member of Die Brücke, and the one who invented the name for the group – the implication was that it provided a link which held the group together, and led into the future – was in some ways more single-minded than either of the other two. For several years figures hardly ever appeared in his paintings. Introverted and reserved, often in a state of latent hostility to some of his fellow-members, his bold vigorous handling, vehement at times to the point of coarseness, his heavily saturated colours and large undefined compositional areas, brought him to the brink of pure abstraction. He was impassioned by the sea, and a determinant influence on his art was the landscape of Norway, which he visited frequently. Emil Nolde (*see below*), whom he introduced to the group, had helped him to achieve that transition from Impressionism which was an almost essential episode in the development of any Expressionist, but it was the move to Berlin, with its wider horizons, its more explicit literary interests, which led him away from landscapes to figures and still-lifes, to a more precise definition of the subject matter, to a more fragmented and complex form of composition, with the landscape reduced to a series of two-dimensional symbols (as in *Summer*) against which the human figures appear as almost primeval statues.

After the war Schmidt-Rottluff's work became more lyrical, less vibrant, and he took refuge in religious transcendentalism from the barbarism of his age, moving to a kind of Symbolism with strong literary and theological undercurrents. This was a common enough pattern at the time. Similar conversions had affected the Decadents and other writers and artists, who, relying initially too much on the absolute validity of their own sensations, had tended to react violently in the opposite direction when the inevitable disillusionment came. Forbidden to paint by the Nazis, who confiscated his works, he was appointed in 1946 to a professorship at the Berlin Hochschule für Bildende Kunst.

Emil Hansen, who in 1901, at the age of thirty-four, changed his name to Nolde, was both the outsider and the professional of Die Brücke. In 1898, while a drawing teacher at St Gallen in Switzerland, he decided to become a full-time painter, and went to study with Adolf Hölzel at a small village near Munich which bore the still-innocent name of Dachau. A Czech by birth, Hölzel was, through his teachings and writings, a figure of seminal significance in the evolution of contemporary art. Deeply interested in problems of colour harmony, preoccupied with using

Karl Schmidt-Rottluff
Summer 1913

Karl Schmidt-Rottluff
Lady with Fruit-dish 1909

natural forms as the basis of a visual vocabulary, his writings had a strong social bias, and he was one of the main contributors to the significantly titled magazine *Die Kunst für Alle* ('Art for All'), which was widely read throughout Europe.

After his contact with Hölzel, Nolde spent some time in Paris, where he was greatly impressed by the works of Daumier and Manet. Gradually his Impressionistic technique widened under the combined influence of Gauguin, Van Gogh and Munch, and by 1904 he was using brilliant colours, laid on with an ecstatic disregard for the conventional techniques of brushwork. These paintings inevitably attracted the attention of the much younger artists of Die Brücke, who asked him to join them, and he took part in the group exhibitions of 1906 and 1907. But he felt that the group was too confined, too inhibiting, and tried to start a rival association, more broadly based, and including Christian Rohlfs, Munch, Matisse, Max Beckmann and Schmidt-Rottluff. This was abortive, and equally unsuccessful was his attempt to take over the leadership of the Neue Sezession in Berlin in 1911. Some forty years later he wrote: 'Munch's work led to the founding of the Berlin Secession, my work to its groups, but when in 1911 one of these rejected his *Last Judgment*, he and Marc founded Der Blaue Reiter, which held a series of exhibitions in Munich and Berlin and published an 'almanac' or year book, *Der Blaue Reiter*, whose one and only issue included essays and reviews about all the arts, and numbered among its contributors Schönberg, Webern and Berg, and among its illustrations, folk art, children's drawings and works by Cézanne, Matisse, Douanier Rousseau, the Brücke group, Van Gogh and Delaunay. Indeed, Der Blaue Reiter was cosmopolitan in its membership and affiliations, including in one or other of these categories Russians such as Mikhail Larionov and Natalia Goncharova; Frenchmen such as Braque, Derain, Picasso and Robert Delaunay; and the Swiss Louis-René Moilliet and Henry Bloè Niestlé.

But, whatever stylistic allegiances Der Blaue Reiter commanded, and however divergent the paths which its members later followed, it was in its conception and short life – the group dispersed in 1914 – essentially German in origin, Expressionist in nature. In the *Prospectus* to the catalogue of the first exhibition at the Thannhauser gallery in Munich we find another statement of those familiar ideals: 'To give expression to inner impulses in every form which provokes an intimate personal reaction in the beholder. We seek today, behind the veil of external appearances, the hidden things which seem to us more important than the discoveries of the Impressionists. We search out and elaborate this hidden side of ourselves not from caprice nor for the sake of being different, but because this is the side we see.'

But by and large, the members of Der Blaue Reiter were more rigorous and more searching in their attitudes than were most of their contemporaries. They investigated colour theories, became concerned with problems of perception, flirted fruitfully with the physical sciences (Kandinsky owed much to the microscope), explored imaginary space and declared their independence of the boundaries of the visible world. Deeply influenced by the philosophical speculations of Wilhelm Worringer, whose *Abstraktion und Einfühling* ('Abstraction and Empathy') was published in 1907, several of them wrote persuasively in creative forms. Their approach to art was interdisciplinary in a way which had not been seen since the Renaissance.

Wassily Kandinsky was born and educated in Russia, and having in 1895 been converted to art by seeing an exhibition of the French Impressionists in Moscow, came to Munich, to devote himself entirely to painting, at a time when that city was the centre of the so-called New Style of art in Germany. He expressed himself in a wide variety of media (forecasting in his concern with the decorative arts his future involvement with the Bauhaus), designing clothing, tapestries and handbags. His painting was at this point predominantly Art Nouveau with Symbolist undercurrents, but already possessing allusive, emotive qualities. Travelling extensively, he was widely recognized, and he received medals in Paris in 1904 and 1905, was elected to the jury of the Salon d'Automne, and won a Grand Prix in 1906.

But during this period stronger, more vital impulses began to be apparent in his work. He digested the influence of Cézanne, Matisse and Picasso; he began to understand the value of Bavarian folk art; his colours began to sing; visible shapes began to lose their descriptive qualities. In paintings such as *On the Outskirts of the City* of 1908 the actual subject matter is of slight importance; indeed, it is positively irrelevant. What matters is the sense of dynamism which controls the cumulus-like groups of strongly contrasting colours; 'Houses and trees made hardly any impression on my thoughts. I used the palette knife to spread lines and splashes of paint on the canvas, and make them sing as loudly as I could. My eyes were filled with the strong saturated colours of the light and air of Munich, and the deep thunder of its shadows.'

This was a crucial moment in the history of modern art. The Dionysiac freedom of Expressionism was being suffused with another element, the metaphysical tradition of Russian Byzantinism, with its strong anti-naturalistic, hieratic tendencies. From 1910 onwards Kandinsky continued painting pictures in which representational elements were still discernible; but side by side with these were works such as the *Large Study* of 1914, in which forms as well as colours have taken off into a world of their own, owing little to any recognizable visual phenomena – even though he did find some difficulty in creating an entirely abstract iconography. In the famous apologia which he published in 1910, *Über das Geistige in der Kunst*, ('Concerning the Spiritual in Art'), he used the word

Wassily Kandinsky
On the Outskirts of the City 1908

Wassily Kandinsky
Large Study 1914

geistig, usually translated as 'spiritual', to describe the unreal elements in his paintings; perhaps today we would incline towards translating it by some adjective involving a suggestion of the psychological. These whirling shapes move across the canvas like dancing Dervishes, suggesting impulses deeper than those 'emotional' impulses which powered the main stream of Expressionism. His subsequent career indicated the extent to which he was constantly motivated by the desire to achieve a synthesis of thought and feeling, science and art, logic and intuition.

All his achievements were rooted in the original liberating experience of Expressionism, but there were others, less cosmopolitan in their upbringing, less vigorous in their empiricism, who never shook off their early dependence on a framework of naturalistic references. Whether this would have been true of Franz Marc it is impossible to say; he was killed at Verdun in his mid thirties, at a moment when he seemed to be reaching a point of evolution which his friend Kandinsky had arrived at a few years earlier. There was a strongly obsessive quality about his imagination, perhaps not unconnected with his religious preoccupations. He had started off as a theology student before turning to painting, which he looked upon as a spiritual rather than a worldly activity. Bowled over by Impressionism, he devoted himself for several years to the study of animal anatomy, and even gave lessons on the subject. Although these studies were undertaken primarily to evolve general principles of form from the close examination of the particular, they assumed a special emotional significance for him in his devotion to the horse – that symbol so loved by advertising agents and adolescent girls. To him animals came to represent a sort of primeval purity, each signifying some admirable strength or desirable virtue: the deer fragile agility, the tiger restrained, latent strength. Although at first he painted animals in the foreground of

Franz Marc
Deer in Wood II 1913–14

Franz Marc
Tiger 1912

August Macke
Lady in a Green Jacket 1913

his pictures, later they became integrated with the landscape, as though he were seeking a complete identification of both.

Having secured expressive forms, he went on, under the influence of his friend August Macke, another member of Der Blaue Reiter, who of all the group came closest to the Fauves, to explore the emotional potentials of colour. 'If you mix red and yellow to make orange, you turn passive yellow into a Fury, with a sensual force that again makes cool spiritual blue indispensable. In fact blue always finds its place inevitably at the side of orange. The colours love each other. Blue and orange make a thoroughly festive sound.'

The sexual undertones, the rather childish symbolism, the strong sense of personalization – all are typical of Marc, and of his generation. His colour experiments were leading to a dissolution of form similar to that being achieved by Kandinsky, when his death cut them short.

Like Kandinsky a Russian by birth, Alexei von Jawlensky was closely associated with Der Blaue Reiter, but did not participate in any of their joint exhibitions. Though he was later to grow close to Nolde, the formative influences on his work up to about 1912 were those of Gauguin, Matisse and Van Dongen. His warm and passionate painting depended largely on simplification, brilliant colours held within dark contours, and a bounding sinuous line, which gives a hieratic unity to the whole composition. The impact of the war led to an exaggeration of that taste

Alexei von Jawlensky
Girl with Peonies 1909

for religious mysticism which he shared with Marc and others. 'Art' he
said 'is nostalgia for God', and after 1917 the bulk of his work consisted of
têtes mystiques – abstract head forms.

Although Expressionism in general, and the Blaue Reiter (in whose
exhibitions he participated) were of great importance in the development
of the art of Paul Klee, his approach to both was tentative, marked by
that sense of hesitation which characterized the whole of his early career.
Right from the beginning he had been, by instinct as it were, a linear
Expressionist, producing graphic forms which paid little attention to
naturalistic conventions, and which were bent or distorted to convey a
sense of whimsical irony, even of gentle sadism – emphasizing the debt
which non-realist art owed to the traditions of caricature. Line for him

was an independent structural element which he deployed to express
strong sensations. But his contacts with Der Blaue Reiter led him to
assume enough courage to explore the potentials of colour. He took the
final step in 1914 when on a trip to Tunisia with Macke and Moilliet. It
was the outcome of a long process rather than a moment of sudden
conversion. In effect, he was an introvert who schooled himself to become
an extrovert, a classicist who turned to romanticism (he always confessed
to preferring Cézanne to Van Gogh). But, even so, it was in the
compromise medium of watercolour that he was happiest, and that he
made the most advances. In works such as *The Föhn Wind in the Marcs'
Garden* of 1915, perfunctory gestures to perspectival space can still be seen,
and he was never completely to renounce references to objective reality;
he regarded it as a source of materials from which to create a personal
imagery rather than as a model to be copied. Complex, subtle and lyrical,
the picture is composed of roughly geometric sections each containing its

Paul Klee
The Föhn Wind in the Marcs' Garden 1915

Alfred Kubin
One-eyed Monster

own colour, the different shapes forming a contrapuntal flat pattern which moves up and across the surface of the paper.

At the opposite pole of Expressionism, but within the same milieu, Alfred Kubin represented a tradition very different from the delicate happy fantasies of Klee. Mainly an illustrator, his imagination was nurtured on the morbid, and he gave shape to the nightmares of anxiety in a style which owed something to Beardsley, something to Goya, and a good deal to Odilon Redon. The author of a strange novel, *Die andere Seite* ('The Other Side'), he reasserted in the twentieth century the 'Gothic' traditions of the early nineteenth.

Der Sturm: Berlin and Vienna

It would be wrong, of course, to think of the experiments of Die Brücke and the Blaue Reiter as the sole manifestations of the new visual romanticism which was sweeping through the German-speaking countries. In both Berlin and Vienna powerful Secession movements – anti-academies, beset by schisms – gathered the progressive elements in the arts into an uneasy alliance. Not all of these elements, even within the

Opposite:

Max Beckmann
Self-portrait with a Red Scarf 1917

Lyonel Feininger
Zirchow V 1916 (detail)

Expressionist idiom, would have subscribed to the radical theories of Kandinsky or Marc, and within the pages of art journals such as Herwarth Walden's *Der Sturm* (which was largely responsible for publicizing the notion of Expressionism as a movement) bitter controversies raged about the extent to which traditional attitudes should be accepted or rejected. A typical figure in this context was that of Max Beckmann, who commenced as an instinctual Expressionist working in a style which owed a good deal to Munch and even to Delacroix, and taking as his themes subjects such as his mother's deathbed, the Messina earthquake of 1910, or the sinking of the *Titanic*. He emphasized, especially in the course of a lengthy controversy with Marc, which appeared in the magazine *Pan* in 1912, the traditional qualities of paint: 'Appreciation for the peach-coloured sheen of skin, the glint of a nail, for what is artistically sensual; for those things such as the softness of flesh, the gradations of space, which lie not only on the surface of a picture, but in its depths. Appreciation too for the attraction of the material. The rich gloss of oil paint which we find in Rembrandt, in Cézanne; the inspired brushwork of Frans Hals.'

A conversion which no aesthetic dialectics could bring about was effected by his traumatic experiences as a medical orderly – experiences which not only caused him to have a nervous breakdown, but also made his style into a medium appropriate for expressing their bitter content. The tormented anguish of the *Self-portrait with a Red Scarf* of 1917 is expressed not only in the appearance of the face and in the pose, but in the cramped space, the acrid colours, the dryness of handling – far removed from his earlier delight in quality of pigment and sensuality of texture. Producing for the rest of his career mainly figure paintings, including many self-portraits, he presented them as symbols of pure despair, essays in existentialist agony.

Lyonel Feininger and Oscar Kokoschka presented differing but complementary antitheses to Beckmann's pessimistic passion; the one was inventive in style, the other predominantly traditionalist; both were much more joyous in content. Feininger, who rejected groups and never participated in a manifesto, openly declared himself an Expressionist: 'Every work I do serves as an expression of my most personal state of mind at that particular moment, and of the inescapable, imperative need for release by means of an appropriate act of creation, in the rhythm, form, colour and mood of the picture.'

In fact, his inspiration derived mainly from the Cubists, and to a lesser degree from the Futurists; it was the first two qualities, rhythm and form, which were most apparent in his work. Geometric in construction, with metamorphosized figurative elements, his works are sharper than those of Robert Delaunay, with which they have considerable affinities. The colour is brooding, the subject matter larger in scale than the average French Cubist would have attempted; the analysis into geometric units is complete and thorough, taking in every element in the painting – including even the light in the sky. It was light which contributed the major Expressionist element to his works, wrapping them in a sense of mystery and drama, making them, despite the austerity of the style, emotionally disturbing.

More self-confident in its hedonistic cosmopolitanism than Berlin, the capital of the Austro-Hungarian empire had experienced in the closing decades of the nineteenth century a Secession movement dominated by the Byzantine sensuality of Gustav Klimt's paintings. The emotionally liberated principles which underlay the movement were disseminated throughout Europe in the pages of the magazine *Ver sacrum* which greatly influenced Die Brücke.

Stylistically Egon Schiele, one of Klimt's pupils, who was briefly imprisoned for producing what were described as 'pornographic' drawings, depended very much on the luscious linear vitality of Klimt's art, but he added to it a pungent morbidity of his own which is heightened by elegant formal distortions. Even his oil paintings have something of the quality of watercolour, and he found special pleasure in this medium, using it originally for subjects with a marked erotic appeal, but later – especially in those works which he produced in prison – expressing a tormented anguish of spirit.

A good deal is often made of the fact that Kokoschka grew up in the Vienna of Sigmund Freud, and his concern with portraiture – rare in the avant-garde of the twentieth century – is often related to his desire to penetrate beneath the disguise of appearance to the sitter's inner

Egon Schiele
Portrait of the Painter Paris von Gütersloh 1918

Egon Schiele
For My Art and for My Loved Ones I Will Gladly Endure to the End! 25 April 1912

Oskar Kokoschka
The Bride of the Wind (The Tempest) 1914

Max Ernst
The Bride of the Wind 1926 27

personality. But the effects which critics tend to attribute to psychological penetration are more likely to have been determined by the stylistic attitudes which he formed in the period between 1910 and 1914 when his thin, tortuous linear patterns were reinforced by a passion for rich, heavy impasto through which figures emerge, and by means of which they are defined. In one of his more famous works of this period, *The Bride of the Wind (Die Windsbraut)*, all the qualities which have made his work so popular and so significant are immediately apparent: an immense capacity for visual rhetoric, which can at times descend to pomposity; an ability to contain within a single composition the most disparate elements; and a sense of Baroque vitality. The historical analogy is significant; for throughout his career Kokoschka basically worked within the framework of traditional Renaissance and post-Renaissance conventions, even favouring the same kind of scale. In *The Bride of the Wind* there are obvious references to El Greco and to Delacroix; the size conforms to that of the *grandes machines* of Rubens or Poussin (it is 181 × 220 cm), and there are no striking innovations in form or construction. What is special to Kokoschka's generation and the Expressionist tradition of art is the apocalyptic treatment of the theme, the morbidity of the colour, and the adaptation of the actual handling of the medium to create a mood.

It is interesting in this connection to compare Kokoschka's painting with one of several which his younger contemporary Max Ernst produced on the same theme – significantly, the Germans use the word *Windsbraut* to mean 'Storm Wind' – in the 1920s. Expressionism had been the force which initially liberated Ernst, and his early works before the war were well within its idiom. But after his encounter with the Nihilism of Dada he turned to the Surrealist liberation of unconscious imagery.

In his *Bride of the Wind* the sense of violence, aggression and disquiet is expressed formally in a style which contains all the basic elements of the Expressionists – emotive colour, turbulent shapes distorted to provoke strong reactions in the spectator – and added to them is a whole series of sexual metaphors, involving the sense of rape, the whole effect heightened by the contrast with the placid lunar circle.

Ernst Barlach
Manifestations of God: The Cathedrals 1922

After the Great War

The political ferment which characterized the post-war years in Germany
gave aesthetic allegiances even stronger political undertones than those
they had already expressed. Powerful though the appeals of Dada and
Futurism were, it was Expressionism which commanded the big aesthetic
battalions, and which became identified most clearly with all the
progressive elements in the tragedy of the Weimar republic. Even the
older painters were inspired by its fervour; and Lovis Corinth, whose
vigorous Impressionism had inspired Nolde and Macke, now abandoned
this for a charged, violent emotional style – with strong social
undercurrents – closer to that of his disciples than to that of his
predecessors.

Lovis Corinth
The Painter Bernd Grönvold 1923

The temper of the times also gave fresh impetus to the interest which
the Expressionists had always shown in graphic media – with their
propaganda potential being transferred from aesthetic to political ends.
The reasons for this interest were many and complex. The stylistic
innovations pioneered by Crane and William Morris; the growing
popularity of illustrated books; the impact of Beardsley, of Gauguin and
of Lucien Pissarro, each of whom in his own way had extended the range
of prints and engravings, was reinforced by a contemporary interest in the
tradition of the popular German woodcut of the late Middle Ages, with
its strong democratic appeal. It was this influence which led artists such
as Nolde, Heckel and Ernst Barlach (1870–1938) to produce works in
black and white, simple in composition, urgent in emotional appeal, with
perspectival effects created by the interrelation of planes, and arrogantly
devoid of any attempt to please or charm.

The desire to rape rather than to seduce the spectator's sensibilities,
which was inherent in many Expressionist works, seemed especially
relevant in the 1920s; and it was seen at its most compelling in an artist
who, though belonging at one point to the Berlin Dadaists, was at heart
committed to the stylistic manners of the Expressionists, using visual
violence to excoriate the establishment and propagate his own democratic

ideas. George Grosz recorded, with a bitter brilliance which has never been excelled, the unacceptable face of capitalism. He produced a flood of lithographs, prints and paintings which document post-war Germany with the same virulent accuracy with which Daumier portrayed the France of Louis-Philippe. But his strength was his weakness, and though his colour could often be gently lyrical, he could never seem to overcome a basic distaste for humanity, despite the democratic ideals which informed his work. He was always best at his most sadistic, and he exemplifies, in an exaggerated form, the strong streak of Puritanical venom which frequently powers the Expressionist imagination.

The Expressionists had led the last attack on the ramparts of rationality, and had breached them. They gave to instinct a standing in the visual arts which the Romantics had never succeeded in establishing; they declared their independence of the visible world, and gave the

George Grosz
Market Scene with Fruits 1934

George Grosz
Gold Diggers 1920

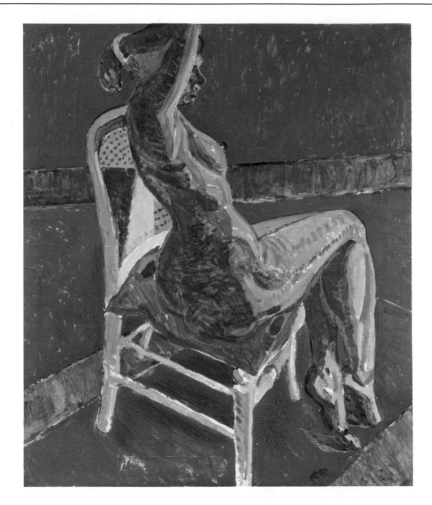

Matthew Smith
Nude, Fitzroy Street, No. 1 1916

subconscious a new significance in the act of creation. The actual
techniques which they had evolved were used by many artists to achieve
effects not dissimilar from those which they themselves sought. The strong
simple colours and passionate vision which characterize the works of a
basically Fauve painter such as Matthew Smith (1879–1959) represent
one aspect of a tradition which complements the more personal emotional
vehemence of an artist such as Jack Yeats, whose concern with a semi-
private mythology echoes through thick layers of luminous paint applied
with a vigorous, whirling brush stroke. Nor would any member of Die
Brücke or Der Blaue Reiter see in the sun-drenched, fiercely expressed
imagery of the Australian Arthur Boyd anything very different from what
he himself had been trying to achieve.

The passion for violence, the search for ultimates in sensation and
feeling which could yet be confined within the traditional framework of
painting are yet another aspect of the legacy of Expressionism, and the
resemblances between Francis Bacon's *Study of Red Pope* and Chaim
Soutine's *Pageboy at Maxim's* are more than fortuitous. Both are motivated
by the desire to express in the resonances of colour, in the deformation of

lines, in the exaggeration of physical characteristics, a sensational impact experienced by the artist, impressed on the spectator.

At the same time, too, as painters had been moving towards a mode of creativity based on the creative significance of passion, so the aestheticians and the critics were providing new theoretical bases for establishing that infallibility of the *id* which was one of the tacit assumptions of the Expressionist approach. John Russell, for instance, sets out to explain (and in a sense to vindicate) Bacon's multi-planed distorted imagery in terms of the notion of 'unconscious scanning' which Anton Ehrenzweig formulated in *The Hidden Order of Art* (1967), and which is a continuation of an Expressionist theory of creativity first formulated by Worringer fifty years earlier. Rationalization, control, restraint, analysis, are converted into psychological sins; spontaneity, the

Chaim Soutine
Pageboy at Maxim's (Le Chasseur d'Hôtel)
1927

rejection of conscious vision, 'the chaos of the subconscious', the undifferentiated structure of subliminal perception, are virtues.

The moralistic undertones are obvious, and this was to be emphasized by the fact that when, with the advent of the New York school of Abstract Expressionism, the critic Clement Greenberg set out to provide it with a rationale, he did so virtually in terms of the notion that, because of the absolute spontaneity of works dictated by pure gestural chance, they achieve a kind of liberating truth which is at once virtuous and therapeutic. And this notion has gone far, spilling over into the conduct of life as 'doing your own thing' and making possible the cult of contemporary culture-heroes such as Joseph Beuys.

Nor are the earlier formal impulses of Expressionism yet exhausted. The *art brut* of a painter such as Jean Dubuffet shows a conscious intention to assault the eye, and he himself has said about the *Corps de Dame* series: 'I have always delighted (and I think this delight is constant

Francis Bacon
Study from Innocent X 1962

Willem De Kooning
Woman and Bicycle 1952–53

in all my paintings) in contrasting in these feminine bodies the extremely general and the extremely particular; the metaphysical and the grotesquely trivial.' Willem De Kooning is one of those who, turning their backs on the earlier purely abstract phases of their careers, have reverted to inspirations which would not have been alien to the early Expressionists.

But to limit the contemporary significance of Expressionism to the occasional survival of its stylistic mannerisms would be to underrate it. More than any other single episode in the history of art during the last century it has emancipated painting, extended the boundaries of form, line and colour, made possible the impossible. Nothing in art that has happened since its beginnings has been untouched by its liberating effect.

4 Cubism, Futurism and Constructivism

J.M. NASH

Cubism, Futurism and Constructivism were the three most important movements in early twentieth-century art. They developed in different places and at different times – Cubism grew up in Paris between 1907 and 1914, Futurism was announced in a manifesto from Milan on 20 February 1909, and Constructivism first flourished in Moscow after the Revolution of 1917 – but there were many links between them. The Futurist painters visited the studios of the Cubists in Paris in 1911 and what they saw there profoundly influenced their style. The Constructivists learned from both earlier movements. Almost all the major artists of the first half of this century were active in one or more of the movements. Between them they created modern art. They created new forms, experimented with new procedures and propounded theories of art that still affect our ideas about the purpose and value of art. But in many ways the movements were strongly opposed to each other. It was not simply that the Cubists dismissed the Futurists as Italian plagiarists – as they did – or that the Italians called Cubism a 'sort of masked academicism' and said their own art was the only truly modern, *dynamic* art, or that, later, the Constructivists wrote that the 'attempts of the Cubists and Futurists to lift the visual arts from the bogs of the past have led only to new delusions'. No doubt much of this abuse sprang from the modern need to appear to be totally original. But it is clear that despite their various similarities, and despite their mutual interest in and indebtedness to each other, the three movements did stand for quite different values, and these values were moral and social as much as aesthetic.

Cubism

Modern art, it has often been said, began with Cubism. Cubism has been called a revolution in the visual arts as great as that which took place in the early Renaissance. Futurism and Constructivism owed it a debt that they disliked having to acknowledge. But unlike Futurism and Constructivism, true Cubism was not conceived as a movement at all. Whatever its other virtues, a movement in art, like a political movement, sets out to confront the larger public. It depends on organized demonstrations for its existence. True Cubism, was, on the contrary, a deliberately private, essentially esoteric art, created by two painters for themselves and for a small circle of intimates.

These painters were Pablo Picasso, who was Spanish, and Georges Braque, who was French. Their circle of friends included a number of

Pablo Picasso
The Three Dancers 1925

whose deformation caused little surprise – we had been prepared for it by
Picasso himself, by Matisse, Derain, Braque . . . and even earlier by
Cézanne and Gauguin. It was the ugliness of the faces that froze with
horror the half-converted.' The Medusa-masks, he says, shocked because
they affronted the Renaissance canons of female beauty.

But Salmon does not explain why Picasso should make this attack. On
the contrary, he stresses the gratuity of the act. 'Picasso', he says, 'at that
time was leading a wonderful life. Never had the blossoming of his free
genius been so radiant . . . he consented to be led by an imagination
quivering with excitement. . . . He had no ground for hoping that some
different effort would bring him more praise or make his fortune sooner,
for his canvases were beginning to be competed for. And yet Picasso felt
uneasy. He turned his pictures to the wall and threw down his brushes.
Through long days – and nights as well – he drew.'

The reason for Picasso's unease can only be guessed at. A possible
source can be discovered within that small circle of friends that revolved
around him. The circle was all-important: not only was it the sole source
of outside acclaim that he could value, but without two of its members,
Gertrude Stein and her brother Leo, he might starve again as he had
before they had discovered him. He was, however, not the Stein's only
protegé. In his copy of the catalogue of the Salon des Indépendants held
in March 1906, Apollinaire scribbled: 'at the moment [Leo] Stein swears
only by two painters, Matisse and Picasso.'

Henri Matisse was thirty-six in 1906, twelve years older than Picasso
and the doyen of the avant-garde. The previous year his paintings had
been displayed at the Salon d'Automne with those of several friends and
they had caused a sensation. Their colouring was improbably bright,
daubed straight from the tube in strokes a child could have made, in the
view of most critics and visitors to the exhibition. A critic, Louis
Vauxcelles, dubbed the group 'Les Fauves', the wild beasts. As the other
painters in the group, André Derain, Maurice de Vlaminck, Albert
Marquet, and Kees van Dongen among them, were all younger than
Matisse, he was called 'the king of the beasts'.

Picasso was a regular visitor at the apartment at 27 rue de Fleurus
where his new patrons lived; and each Saturday, when he went to dinner,
he would see these advanced and admired paintings and often would
meet Matisse himself. When, later in 1906, he began making studies for a
large and unconventional painting of female nudes, he must have realized
it would be at once compared with Matisse's works, and with two
canvases in particular: *The Happiness of Living* (*Le Bonheur de vivre*), owned
by the Steins, and the *Luxury, Calm and Delight* (*Luxe, calme et volupté*) that
had been the centrepiece of the Salon d'Automne of 1905. The latter,
painted in the Pointillist technique, with prismatically bright spots of
colour, represented a group of naked and half-naked women bathing and
picnicking on the seashore. The *Bonheur de vivre* was even more
outrageously bold. In colour and general effect it was more like a Persian
carpet than a traditional European oil painting. Its drawing was as free
as its colouring and suggested eighteenth-century Japanese woodcuts.

In these two ambitious paintings, Matisse had undertaken the strangest
subject of nineteenth-century painting: the grand composition of female

nudes. In Paris, in the nineteenth century, in the great exhibition halls of the annual Salons, to which bourgeois families flocked in thousands each weekend, the nude composition flourished in an astounding way. Venus, Galatea, Diana, minor inhabitants of Olympus, nymphs, and many other subjects were given as titles, but it was clear that the subject was becoming less and less important. But when it was stripped even of its subject matter, the nakedness of the nude composition became more problematic. If the critic's general impression was that it was 'acceptable', it was praised for its execution, the excellence of its draughtsmanship, the delicacy of its colouring, and also for the beauty of its subject. If not, drawing, colouring and the ugliness of the model might be criticized, but it was probable that the picture would be finally condemned as objectionable, vulgar or indecent.

There were two artists of the nineteenth century who, by 1906, were at once heroic in their genius and inevitably associated with compositions of nudes. The one whose influence on Cubism is unmistakable is Paul Cézanne. His late paintings of women bathing, often thought to be the climax of his career, have been taken to be important influences on Picasso when he was creating the *Demoiselles*. Cézanne died in 1906, and his achievement was recognized as the greatest in contemporary art.

The other painter of the nude was the old master, Jean-Dominique Ingres, 'the great painter, the artful adorer of Raphael' as his contemporary Charles Baudelaire had called him in 1845. Among his many paintings of the female nude, one was unprecedented. This was the *Turkish Bath* (*Le Bain turc*) of 1863, finished when he was eighty-two. This

Pablo Picasso
Study for *Les Demoiselles d'Avignon* 1907

Pablo Picasso
Les Demoiselles d'Avignon 1907

one foreshortened thigh. The other sketch shows the same contour modified first into a front view of a torso, then into another similar face, but this time the eyes are the breasts and the mouth is equated with the female genitals. It is an equation that occurred in several of Goya's *Caprichos*.

This is the Medusa mask that 'froze with horror the half-converted', as Salmon observed. It is an aesthetic indecency that metaphorically transfers the obscene display, originally made to the sailor, directly to the spectator. The painting did not lose its original subject. Salmon says that it was at once named *The Philosophical Brothel*; he named it after the Carrer d'Avinyò, a street in the Barcelona red-light area.

If Picasso's canvas was a response to Matisse's *Happiness of Living* – a modern version of Ingres' *Turkish Bath* – it was a cruel one. The only explanation given by anyone likely to know is that given by Salmon, who simply said that Picasso took savage artists as his mentors because 'his logic led him to think that their aim had been the genuine representation of a being, not the realization of the idea we have of it'. He has taken Ingres's dream of houris, swooning languorously in an Oriental bathhouse, and given it the *realistic* savagery of a 'truly' primitive style.

Matisse and Leo Stein were very angry when they saw the *Demoiselles*. They laughed and said Picasso was trying to create fourth dimension. It was at this time that Georges Braque was brought on his first visit to the Bateau Lavoir. When he saw the *Demoiselles* he too was shocked. He said to Picasso: 'Despite all your explanations, you paint as if you wanted us to eat rope-ends or to drink petrol.'

Braque was only six months younger than Picasso, but he was not a prodigy. It was at the Salon des Indépendants held in March 1907 (when Picasso was already at work on the *Demoiselles*) that he had his first professional success. He sold all six pictures he was exhibiting. His work was noticed by a young German dealer, Daniel-Henry Kahnweiler, who had just opened a gallery in Paris. That October, he signed a contract to buy Braque's entire production. He also introduced him to Apollinaire. Apollinaire naturally introduced him to Picasso.

Whatever Braque thought of the *Demoiselles* when he first saw it, it must have made a profound impression on him. The paintings with which he had been so successful at the Salon des Indépendants that Spring had been Fauve, but soon after his visit to Picasso's studio he began to work on a quite different subject and kind of painting. This was a medium-sized painting of a nude which occupied him for the following six months. Everything about this painting suggests that after seeing the *Demoiselles* he set out deliberately to transform his way of painting.

The influence of the *Demoiselles* can be seen in many features of Braque's *Nude*. Most striking is the empty-eyed mask which is turned to stare blankly at the spectator over a shoulder. The vigorous outlines, too, suggest the *Demoiselles*' effect. Like the *Demoiselles*, it is placed against drapery that is sculpted into hard, angular folds. And just as in Picasso's invention, the spatial orientation is obscure. The Demoiselle in the pink peignoir draws back a brown curtain to reveal a milky blue sky which is itself a curtain parted to reveal another darker interior. The Demoiselle with one arm raised was, in the earliest drawings, sitting on a chair. Now she appears to stand, or rather to slide to one side; her pose is almost the same as that of the famous Venus painted in sixteenth-century Venice by Giorgione, that now known as the Dresden Venus, except that Giorgione's Venus is lying down. Braque's nude looks most uncomfortably balanced on the toes of her right foot, but appears much more at ease as if she is seen lying down, shown from above. Nothing allows the spectator to make a decision between these possibilities.

Despite its striking kinship with the *Demoiselles*, Braque's *Nude* marks the beginning of Cubism in a way that Picasso's picture does not. For much of 1908, Picasso followed the implications of his inventions of 1906. His preoccupations were with solid, sculptural forms and bold shapes. This time has been called his 'Negro' period, and even the works which do not resemble African art are *primitive* in their harshness and crudity. Braque, on the other hand, developed from his *Nude* in a different direction. Throughout 1908, he showed, more and more strikingly, the influence of Cézanne. It was Braque's work of 1908 that was first called 'Cubist'. This was by Matisse, who was one of the jury that rejected all the new paintings Braque submitted to the Salon d'Automne of that year. Despite this, these canvases were shown, at Kahnweiler's gallery, that October. Louis Vauxcelles noted that Braque reduced everything to cubes.

Perhaps it was from that time that Picasso began to regard Braque's work seriously. Certainly it was from then that Cubism began to grow.

Georges Braque
Nude 1907–08

Georges Braque
Landscape at L'Estaque 1908

Between then and 1914, the work of Picasso and Braque passed through several transformations, and in retrospect these developments look inevitable, even logical. But true Cubism, this painting of Picasso and Braque, was not the result of a programme, a project. It flourished out of the friendship and rivalry of these two. Braque described the following years: 'We lived in Montmartre, we saw each other every day, we talked. During those years Picasso and I discussed things which nobody will ever discuss again, which nobody else would know how to discuss, which nobody else would know how to understand.' In his memorable phrase, he and Picasso were like 'two mountaineers roped together'. There came a moment when they had difficulty in distinguishing between their paintings. They valued this similarity and abandoned signing their works on the front, leaving it to the assistant of their dealer, Kahnweiler, to identify the work on the back only.

Braque, in the landscapes painted at L'Estaque in 1908, crystallized the essential qualities of Cubism. From Cézanne, Braque learned a good deal. He learned, first of all, to avoid strong diagonals, foreshortening and other perspectival devices that would give clear indications of depth in the traditional way of Western painting. He learned to see or invent patterns in which objects in quite different planes in three dimensions could be balanced two-dimensionally. For example, a tree rising on the right of a canvas will be balanced by a path on the left, and these two curved shapes will between them bracket the landscape. A third device that Braque adapted from Cézanne was to avoid closed contours, to leave gaps in outlines: this allowed objects in quite different planes to melt into each other as they were juxtaposed in the pictorial composition; and it also emphasized the independence of the outline as a pictorial element.

Braque's landscapes were quite unlike those of Cézanne in two significant ways. Cézanne learned from the Impressionists, and his canvases glowed with sunlight; Braque's palette was almost monochromatic (perhaps in reaction against his Fauve days), and he often used a neutral grey. Cézanne's outline was quivering, tentative; Braque drew with an aggressive, bold stroke. Cézanne seemed to contemplate the world, searching for its significance; Braque remade the world as his art demanded it.

From early in 1909, the differences between Picasso's 'Negro' style and Braque's post-Cézanne style diminished and disappeared. They created an art which was, as critics had said of Matisse's Fauvism, theoretical and artificial, but which, unlike Fauve painting, seemed to be about the *substance* of things. Much later, Braque was explicit about his interest in abandoning traditional perspective: 'It was too mechanical to allow one to take full possession of things.' It is a paradox of much Cubist painting, and especially that of Braque, that though it is often hard to know *what* is represented, or even *where* it is meant to be, that unknown, uncertain object is undeniably tangible.

There is no mystery about this. It is the result of the Cubist use of the *facet* as the basic element of painting. This had been Picasso's fundamental technical innovation in the *Demoiselles d'Avignon*. The facet, not the cube, is the key to this art. The facet may vary in size, but its basic features survive from 1908 to 1913. It is a small area bordered by straight or curved lines, two adjacent edges defined with a light tone and two opposite edges with a dark tone, and the area between modulating between these extremes. The tonal effect would suggest a strongly convex or concave surface, but this is denied by the edges of the facet.

The facets are composed according to three principles. First, they are almost always painted as if at a slight angle to the vertical surface of the canvas; that is to say, they are like louvres of a window that are usually ajar, but never fully opened at right-angles to the frame. Secondly, although the facets overlap and cast shadows on each other, the shadows and overlappings are inconsistent; it would be impossible to construct a relief model of a Cubist painting. Thirdly, the edges of facets dissolve, allowing their contents to leak into each other in the manner the Cubists had learnt from Cézanne.

Georges Braque
Still-life with Herrings (Still-life with Fish)
c. 1909–11

Georges Braque
Still-life with Violin and Pitcher 1909–10

Thus these facets, apparently in low relief, painted in traditional chiaroscuro, and so tangible, real, are structured in a baffling paradoxical system that defies immediate identification. Nevertheless, they do represent very real, commonplace objects, pipes, bottles, musical instruments, the possessions of the artists' lives – or are even portraits of their friends and mistresses.

The first phase of Cubism was that created by the fusion of Picasso's primitivism with Braque's post-Cézanne forms. This was the time of bold simplifications into heavy blocks of form. Its monumentality was lightened by the ambiguity of the shapes and by avoidance of the foreshortening that would have given the objects a convincing three-dimensional existence.

Out of this sculptural imagery grew the paradoxical figures of 1910. In this phase unmistakably solid objects were represented in spaces that often appeared profound. But the dimensions of objects and spaces are uncertain, even elusive. In the Tate Gallery, London, are two paintings from this time, a *Seated Nude* by Picasso and *Still-life with Herrings* by Braque. Each painting conveys a strong sense of deep space, of the shifting light and shade of a gloomy studio interior; but each is obscure in

Pablo Picasso
Seated Nude 1909–10

Pablo Picasso
Girl with Mandoline 1910

other ways. Braque's still-life might, at first sight, be a landscape with factory chimneys. Certainly the herrings of the title are hard to identify immediately. Some major forms in the painting never resolve themselves, are irresoluble. But the space in which these objects are suspended, the light that flows about them like a sluggish, ebbing tide – *these* are pictorial forms compelling in their presence.

Picasso's *Seated Nude* of 1910 is enigmatic in another way. The canvas is covered with intersecting diagonals of lighter and darker paint of sombre tones. The surface is homogeneous and yet it is not difficult to identify the figure sitting in a chair and, beyond her shoulder, the distant clutter of a studio. The chair, like the table on which Braque's *Still-life with Herrings* is placed, is drawn in conventional perspective. But the torso framed by its arms is harshly defined, as if assembled perfunctorily from old picture frames and the discarded wooden stretchers of old canvases. It is the head that is totally ambiguous: is it raised to stare out beyond the spectator's left shoulder, or lowered in reverie?

By this time, Picasso and Braque had developed an alternative process of representation that was as flexible and expressive as that of the schools. This may be seen by comparing the Tate Gallery *Seated Nude* with

Pablo Picasso
Ambroise Vollard 1909–10

Pablo Picasso
Daniel-Henry Kahnweiler 1910

the exhibition and demonstration of Futurist art held in Paris in February 1912.

The majority were minor talents, and had they not taken part in the movement would seldom be remembered. These include Gleizes, Metzinger, Herbin, Le Fauconnier, Lhote, Marcoussis and other even lesser figures. There were also artists of real stature who were young enough to pass through Cubism as a form of adolescence before discovering their own styles. The most important of these were Robert Delaunay, Marcel Duchamp and Fernand Léger, though innumerable painters of all nationalities, artists as different as Chagall and Klee, also felt the influence of Cubism.

This leaves André Derain and Juan Gris. Derain had been a powerful innovator among the Fauves. He was one of Picasso's circle, and there is no doubt that in 1907 he looked a daring and original artist. However, though he painted a number of works which show the influence of Cézanne, he never painted anything that might properly be called Cubist. As I have suggested earlier, it was Apollinaire who out of friendship suggested that Derain had played a major role in the creation of Cubism. Juan Gris, a Spaniard six years younger than Picasso, has

Robert Delaunay
The City, no. 2 1910

Fernand Léger
Contrasts of Forms 1913

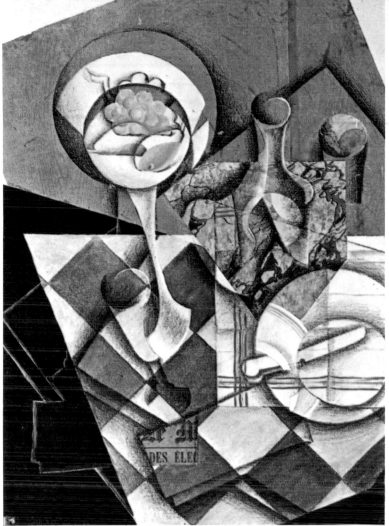

Juan Gris
Sunblind 1914

Juan Gris
Still-life with Fruit and Bottle of Water 1914

been called the third of the true Cubists, but in my view this is unwarranted. He did know Picasso well, he lived in the Bateau Lavoir, and he was certainly talented: he was a better Cubist than any other follower. Between 1913 and 1915, he painted works incorporating collage that could be placed beside the most brilliant of Picasso's works of those years. But his later works became mannered and repetitive, reducing the spontaneity and wit that had been the heart of true Cubism to elegant decoration.

Futurism

Futurism was a movement: it lived on publicity. It was announced in a manifesto published in French on the front page of the Paris newspaper *Le Figaro* on 20 February 1909, while hundreds of copies in Italian were sent to leading figures all over Italy. Between then and the outbreak of the First World War, over a dozen further manifestos were published and were accompanied by countless articles in the press. During the same period, there were Futurist demonstrations and exhibitions in theatres and galleries at towns throughout Italy and in Paris, London, Berlin, based on the study of multiple-exposure photographs. *Rhythm of a Violinist* is similar, but the use of prismatic strokes of colour to represent the disintegration of the hand into a vibrating pattern of lines is ingenious. *Girl Running on a Balcony* is more than ingenious. It too is unmistakably derived from Marey's photographs, but Balla dissolved the entire surface into a mosaic of coloured dabs in the Neo-Impressionist manner. In this way the spectator has simultaneously to form the dabs into a single figure (the girl) and see the girl as moving (in several blurred stages) across the balcony. Finally, there is a neat contrast between the repeated representations of the parts of the girl, each of which is the same individual at different points of time, and the repeated verticals which are different railings stationary at different points in space. Even his later paintings of swifts in flight (taken again from Marey), and of an automobile in movement, are simply heightened sequels to this image. Quite different, and altogether strange, are the series of totally abstract paintings of 1912, the *Iridescent Interpenetrations*, which he developed out of his study of light and colour.

   Despite his seniority, or perhaps because of it, Balla was not representative of Futurist painting at any time. Perhaps the first impressively Futurist paintings were by Carlo Carrà. *The Swimmers* of 1910 and *Leaving the Theatre* of 1910–11 are his first inventions, but his most complete painting came with the *Funeral of the Anarchist Galli* of 1910–11. Angelo Galli had been killed during the general strike in Milan in 1904. Carrà had seen the riot that had developed at his funeral, when clashes between police and workers had almost knocked the red-draped coffin to the ground. In his painting he represents the fight not as a moment between individuals but as a clash of lines and colours. The figures are anonymous and their limbs blur into sheaves of lines

Giacomo Balla
Dynamism of a Dog on a Leash 1912

Giacomo Balla
Rhythm of a Violinist 1912

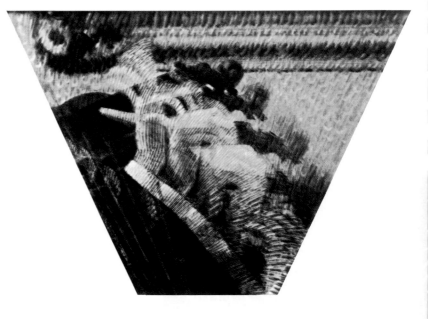

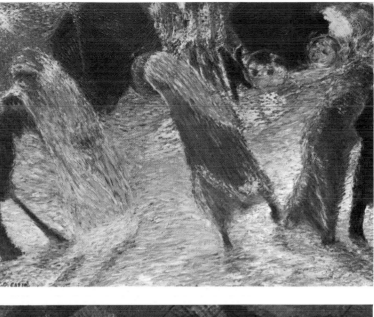

Carlo Carrà
The Swimmers 1910

Carlo Carrà
Leaving the Theatre 1910–11

Carlo Carrà
Funeral of the Anarchist Galli 1911 (detail)

Giacomo Balla
Girl Running on a Balcony 1912

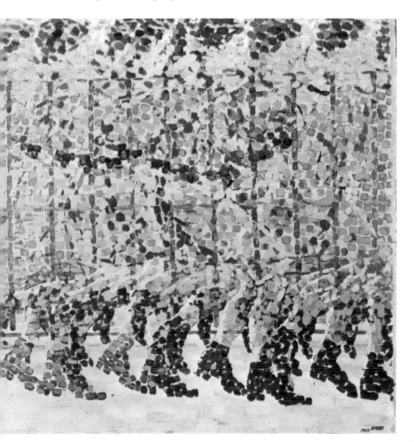

pointed out that perception and experience were not instantaneous. Memory played a fundamental role in our experience, which was inevitably extended over time. *Memories of a Night* and *Solidity of Fog* blend such effects of the persistence of vision as are instanced in the 'Manifesto of the Futurist Painters' within a larger panorama.

It was during 1911 that several of the Futurist painters visited Paris. The reason seems to have been that Gino Severini, a signatory of the manifestos, who lived in Paris, persuaded the others that their work would improve if they could visit the studios of the Cubists. Whatever the reason, late in the year, Boccioni and Carrà went to Paris, and Severini introduced them to his friends and acquaintances as well as taking them to the Salon d'Automne where there were works by Metzinger, Gleizes, Léger, Le Fauconnier, La Fresnaye and others. They also visited Picasso's studio, where they met Apollinaire, who recorded the visit in his gossip column in the *Mercure de France*.

'I have met two Futurist painters, M. Boccioni and M. Severini. . . . These gentlemen wear clothes of English cut, very comfortable. M. Severini, a native of Tuscany, favours low shoes and socks of different colours. . . . This Florentine coquetry exposes him to the risk of being thought absent-minded, and he told me that café waiters often feel obliged to call his attention to what they suppose is an oversight, but which is actually an affectation. I have not yet seen any Futurist paintings, but, if I have correctly understood what the new Italian painters are aiming at in their experiments, they are concerned above all with expressing feelings, almost states of mind (the term was employed by M. Boccioni himself). . . . Furthermore, these young men want to move away from natural forms and to be the inventors of their art.

'"So," M. Boccioni told me, "I have painted two pictures, one expressing departure and the other arrival. The scene is a railway station. In order to emphasize the difference of moods I have not repeated in the arrival picture a single line in the other."'

Apollinaire thought that this kind of painting 'would seem to be above all sentimental and rather puerile'.

Boccioni was, as Apollinaire discovered, the theoretician of the group. He was also the most talented. Nevertheless, he was (with the exception of his teacher Balla) the last of the painters to develop a distinctive Futurist form. He was a year younger than Picasso. For a short time, in 1901, he studied with Severini in Balla's studio in Rome, and his early work shows Balla's influence, particularly in his use of a Neo-Impressionist palette. Many of the drawings he made when he was in his middle twenties have something of the harsh solidity of early drawings by Van Gogh. He was, until 1908, an able but unoriginal member of the Italian Neo-Impressionist school that included Balla, Segantini and Previati.

It was then that he apparently became dissatisfied with this tradition of Impressionist realism. He began to explore the varieties of modernism which, as they were available to him, were forms of Art Nouveau and Symbolism. It was then that he discovered Marinetti and Futurism. Boccioni's first Futurist works illustrate that the movement was essentially an attitude to life. Using a variety of techniques – drawn from Neo-

Umberto Boccioni
The City Rises 1910

Umberto Boccioni
States of Mind I: The Farewells 1911

Umberto Boccioni
The Noises of the Street Invade the House 1911

The railroad took the Russians to the West not only to see but to be seen. In 1906, Serge Diaghilev was the organizer of a Russian section at the Salon d'Automne. It was an exhibition that began with medieval icons and ended with the work of the Moscow avant-garde.

The most talented of the young Russian painters represented at the Salon d'Automne of 1906 were Mikhail Larionov and Natalia Goncharova. Both were born in 1881, the same year as Picasso. They met as students in Moscow and soon became leaders of the avant-garde there. They were equally influenced by the advanced art of the West and the primitivism of Russian icons and folk art. They were inspired by Cubism and the Futurist manifestos; and when, in 1913, Larionov issued a manifesto for a new style he called Rayonnism, it had a distinctly Futurist ring: 'We declare the genius of our days to be: trousers, jackets, shoes, tramways, buses, aeroplanes, railways, magnificent ships. . . . We deny that individuality has any value in a work of art. . . . Hail nationalism! – we go hand in hand with house-painters. . . . Here begins the true freeing of art: a life which proceeds only according to the laws of painting as an independent entity.'

But in 1914 Larionov and Goncharova left Russia to join Diaghilev as designers for his ballet. They never lived again in Russia or contributed to the vital years that followed.

Natalia Goncharova
The Cyclist 1912–13

Mikhail Larionov
Portrait of a Woman 1911

The achievements of the next years were largely those of two rivals, Kasimir Malevich and Vladimir Tatlin. Malevich, the son of a foreman in a sugar factory in Kiev, was largely self-educated. He studied art at the Kiev School of Art, but was twenty-seven before he came to Moscow in 1905, soon to be discovered by Larionov's circle. Between 1909 and 1914, Malevich developed rapidly. From a kind of proto-Cubism, recalling the work of Léger as much as that of Picasso, he passed through a sequence of phases that led him, in 1913, to a type of fragmented collage (anticipating the Dada images of Kurt Schwitters as much as those of Picasso) that he called 'nonsense realism'. These were brilliantly witty, even surreal images, but he quickly moved beyond them – almost inadvertently, it might seem – when he was the designer for Kruchenikh's Futurist opera *Victory over the Sun* (*Pobeda nad Solntsem*) of 1913. The costumes were witty Cubist-Futurist concepts, not quite as outrageous as those Picasso created a few years later for the ballet *Parade*; but it was one of the backcloths that was significant for Malevich. This was simply a square divided into black and white triangles. From this image, Malevich claimed, he moved

Kasimir Malevich
The Knife-Grinder 1912

Kasimir Malevich
An Englishman in Moscow 1914

5 *Dada and Surrealism*

DAWN ADES

Dada

The bourgeois regarded the Dadaist as a dissolute monster, a
revolutionary villain, a barbarous Asiatic, plotting against his bells, his
safe-deposits, his honours list. The Dadaist thought up tricks to rob the
bourgeois of his sleep. . . . The Dadaist gave the bourgeois a sense of
confusion and distant, yet mighty rumbling, so that his bells began to
buzz, his safes frowned, and his honours list broke out in spots.

(*The Navel Bottle* by Hans Arp)

TO THE PUBLIC
Before going down among you to pull out your decaying teeth, your
running ears, your tongues full of sores,
   Before breaking your putrid bones,
   Before opening your cholera-infested belly and taking out for use as
fertilizer your too fatted liver, your ignoble spleen and your diabetic
kidneys,
   Before tearing out your ugly sexual organ, incontinent and slimy,
   Before extinguishing your appetite for beauty, ecstasy, sugar,
philosophy, mathematical and poetic metaphysical pepper and
cucumbers,
   Before disinfecting you with vitriol, cleansing you and shellacking you
with passion,
   Before all that,
   We shall take a big antiseptic bath,
   And we warn you
   We are murderers.
(Manifesto signed by Ribemont-Dessaignes and read by seven people at
the demonstration at the Grand Palais des Champs Elysées, Paris,
5 February 1920).

You are all indicted; stand up! Stand up as you would for the *Marseillaise*
or *God Save the King*. . . .
   Dada alone does not smell: it is nothing, nothing, nothing.
   It is like your hopes: nothing.
   like your paradise: nothing.
   like your idols: nothing.
   like your politicians: nothing.
   like your heroes: nothing.

René Magritte
Natural Graces 1963

like your artists: nothing.
like your religions: nothing.

Hiss, shout, kick my teeth in, so what? I shall still tell you that you are half-wits. In three months my friends and I will be selling you our pictures for a few francs.

(*Manifeste cannibale dada* by Francis Picabia, read at the Dada soirée at the Théâtre de la Maison de l'Œuvre, Paris, 27 March 1920.)

The Dadaists believed that the artist was the product, and, traditionally, the prop, of bourgeois society, itself anachronistic and doomed. The war finally demonstrated its rottenness, but instead of being able to join in the construction of something new, the artist was still trapped in that society's death throes. He was thus an anachronism whose work was totally irrelevant, and the Dadaists wanted to prove its irrelevance in public. Dada was an expression of frustration and anger. But the Dadaists were after all painters and poets, and they subsisted in a state of complex irony, calling for the collapse of a society and its art on which they themselves were still in many ways dependent, and which, to compound the irony, had shown itself masochistically eager to embrace Dada and pay a few sous for its work in order to turn them into Art too.

The Dadaists wrote innumerable manifestos, each one colouring the concept of Dada according to his temperament. But how else can you express frustration and anger? Dada turned in two directions, on the one hand to a nihilistic and violent attack on art, and on the other to games, masks, buffoonery. 'What we call Dada is a harlequinade made of nothingness in which all higher questions are involved, a gladiator's gesture, a play with shabby debris, an execution of postured morality and plenitude', Hugo Ball wrote in his diary, *Die Flucht aus der Zeit*. Picabia and Man Ray produced perfect Dada works of aggression in objects like Picabia's *Portrait of Cézanne*, a stuffed monkey, or Man Ray's *Gift*, an ordinary flat iron with sharp tacks stuck on the bottom, which, combined with Duchamp's suggestion for a Reciprocal Readymade: 'Use a Rembrandt as an ironing board', functions as a metaphor for Dada.

Art had become a debased currency, just a matter for the connoisseur, whose taste was merely dependent on habit. Jacques Vaché, who died of an overdose of opium in 1918 before he had even heard of Dada, but whose flamboyant character and letters full of ironic despair, and humour, were powerful influences on the future Paris Dadaists, wrote to his friend André Breton in 1917: 'ART does not exist, of course – so it is useless to sing – however! we make art because it is thus and not otherwise – . . . So we like neither ART, nor artists (down with Apollinaire) AND HOW RIGHT TOGRATH WAS TO ASSASSINATE THE POET!' Picabia wrote disrespectfully in *Jésus-Christ Rastaquouère*: 'You are always looking for already-felt emotions, just as you like to get an old pair of trousers back from the cleaners, which seem new when you don't look too closely. Artists are cleaners, don't let yourself be taken in by them. True modern works of art are made not by artists but quite simply by men.' Or even, he might have said, by machines.

When Marcel Duchamp in 1913 mounted a bicycle wheel upside down on a stool, and in 1914 chose the first readymade, a bottle-rack, from the

Bazaar de l'Hôtel de Ville, it was the first step in a debate that Dada was to do much to foster – did this gesture of the artist elevate the ordinary mass-produced object into a work of art, or was it like a Trojan Horse, penetrating the ranks of art in order to reduce all objects and works of art to the same level? Of course these are really two sides of the same coin. Anyway, at first the readymades just lay around in his studio, and when he moved to New York in 1915 his sister threw away the *Bottlerack* with the rest of his accumulated rubbish. (He chose another one later.) He only gave them the name Readymade in America, where he began to 'designate' more manufactured objects. Duchamp himself was quite clear that the point was not to turn them into works of art. He explained that the choice of readymade 'depended on the object in general. It was necessary to resist the "look". It is very difficult to choose an object because after a couple of weeks you begin to like it or hate it. You must

Marcel Duchamp
Bicycle Wheel 1913

play chess. His silence was perhaps the most forceful and disquieting of all Dada myths. However, after his death in 1968, it was revealed that he had spent over twenty years, 1944–66, secretly working on an assemblage, a room called *Etant donnés: 1 La chute d'eau, 2 Le gaz d'éclairage*, also traceable back to the *Large Glass* notes.

Duchamp and Francis Picabia had met and immediately became close friends at the end of 1910. Picabia was ebullient, rich and totally nihilistic, and liked the grotesque humour of Alfred Jarry. Duchamp was withdrawn, ironical and esoteric in his tastes. Both were looking for a way out of being trapped and type-cast among the Paris avant-garde, which was predominantly Cubist, and both had an extreme distaste for reverential attitudes towards the 'special nature' of the artist. In 1911, shortly after making contact with the avant-garde's chief spokesman, the poet Guillaume Apollinaire, they attended a performance of Raymond Roussel's *Impressions d'Afrique* which seemed to them a monument of absurd humour. Among the incredible collection of objects and machines (which foreshadow the best Surrealist objects) is a painting machine, activated by rays of sunlight, which of its own accord paints a masterpiece. Roussel's demystification of the work of art, and his systematic destruction of order by pursuit of the absurd, strengthened

Francis Picabia
Parade amoureuse 1917

Francis Picabia
Title-page for *Dada 4/5* 1919

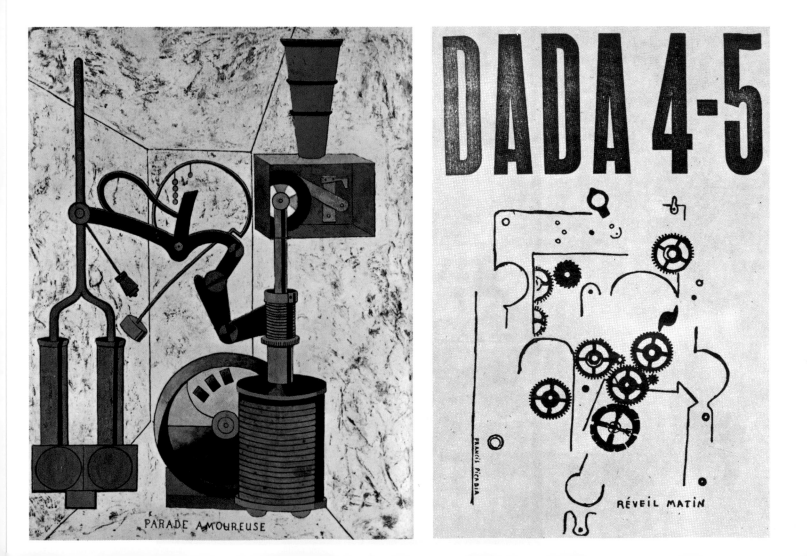

Man Ray
The Rope Dancer Accompanies Herself with Her Shadows 1916

their own similar aims, while the bizarre linguistic games which Roussel describes as the genesis of many of his ideas and objects in *Comment j'ai écrit certains de mes livres* are not unlike the esoteric way in which Duchamp set about constructing his works.

Francis Picabia began making machine drawings under the influence of Duchamp, developing the blasphemous potential of the sex/machine metaphor. He carried the machine drawing to its logical conclusion in 1919 in Zurich when, fittingly, he dismembered a watch, dipped the parts in ink and printed them (title page of *Dada* 4–5). He had published his first machine drawing in Alfred Stieglitz's magazine *Camera Work* at the time of the Armory Show in New York in 1913. The Armory Show had been the first real taste of advanced European art for the American public, and the uproar had centred on a painting by Duchamp, *Nude Descending a Staircase*, so Duchamp was already notorious in New York when, in 1915, both he and Picabia arrived there from Europe. Picabia was furnished with a military commission and money to buy molasses from Cuba, which he immediately put out of his mind. They joined a group of equally insurrectionary poets and painters including John Covert and Man Ray. Arthur Cravan was there intermittently. He had been, in Paris, author of some vitriolic pamphlets, *Maintenant*, and once challenged the ex-heavyweight champion of the world, Jack Johnson, to a disastrous fight in Barcelona, and escaped with his fee. Duchamp and his new aesthetic: gymnastic poem, concert of vowels, bruitist poem, static poem chemical arrangement of ideas, Biriboom, biriboom . . . vowel poem a a ò, i e o, a i i. . . .'

A similar evening culminated in Ball's reading of his new abstract phonetic poem, *O Gadji Beri Bimba*. Encased in a tight-fitting cylinder of shiny blue cardboard, with a high blue and white striped 'witch-doctor's hat', he had to be carried up to the platform. As he began to declaim the sonorous sounds, the audience exploded in laughing, clapping, cat-calls. Ball stood his ground, and, raising his voice above the uproar, began to intone, 'taking on the age-old cadence of priestly lamentation: *zimzim uralalla zimzim urallala zimzim zanzibar zimzalla zam*.'

It was as if he were illustrating his description of Dada in his diary *Die Flucht aus der Zeit*: 'What we are celebrating is at once a buffoonery and a requiem mass. . . . The bankruptcy of ideas having destroyed the concept of humanity to its very innermost strata, the instincts and hereditary backgrounds are now emerging pathologically. Since no art, politics or religious faith seems adequate to dam this torrent, there remain only the *blague* and the bleeding pose.'

Dada works have their only real existence as gestures, public statements of provocation. Whether at exhibitions or demonstrations (and the distinction between them as far as Dada was concerned was deliberately blurred), the Dada object, painting or construction was an act which expected a definite reaction.

Inevitably, some of the experiments of the Dadaists in poetry and the plastic arts seem to some extent to be borrowing the voices of other movements. Hans Richter's *Visionary Self-portrait* is an Expressionist work. Above all, Dada is full of echoes of Italian Futurism, in the violent language of its manifestos, and in its experiments with noise (bruitism) and with simultaneity. George Grosz's Dadaist *Funeral Procession, Dedicated to Oscar Panizza* of 1917, like the Futurist Carlo Carrà's painting *Funeral of the Anarchist Galli* (1911), suggests a funeral that has become a riot. Its dynamic criss-crossing lines and the interpenetrating houses, lights and people also owe a great deal to Umberto Boccioni's more sophisticated concept of simultaneity. Arp referred, in Futurist terms, to the 'dynamic boomboom' of the strong diagonals in his early abstract collages. Arthur Segal's hectic *Harbour*, with its parodied Cubist facets, owes a great deal to Futurism. Very often a style, a device is borrowed in order to satirize itself, to be turned into a grotesque parody. Tzara's 'Simultaneist Poem' is an example – a poem composed of banal verses in three languages, read simultaneously to the accompaniment of noises offstage, mimicking the idea of expressing simultaneous impressions. The Futurists' serious and optimistic attempts at portraying the dynamism, or heroism, of modern life were easy prey for the Dadaists, who regarded this particular branch of artistic activity as the most futile of all.

There was, however, a gulf between the artist in the privacy of his own studio and the same person joining in Dada's public activities. Marcel Janco, for instance, was experimenting with purely abstract plaster reliefs and at the same time making masks for the Dada demonstrations, which Arp remembers happily in 'Dadaland': 'They were terrifying, most of them daubed with bloody red. Out of cardboard paper, horsehair, wire

George Grosz
Funeral Procession, Dedicated to Oskar Panizza
1917

Marcel Janco
Dada, Military Armour 1918–20

and cloth, you made your languorous foetuses, your lesbian sardines, your ecstatic mice.'

Arp was one of the group's most loyal members; although he had little taste for the violence and noise of the Cabaret, he had a very definite idea of the value and meaning of Dada. In this respect he was very close to Hugo Ball. In an essay called 'I become more and more removed from aesthetics' he wrote, 'Dada aimed to destroy the reasonable deceptions of man and recover the natural and unreasonable order. Dada wanted to replace the logical nonsense of the men of today by the illogically senseless. That is why we pounded with all our might on the big drum of Dada and trumpeted the praises of unreason. Dada gave the Venus de Milo an enema and permitted Laocoon and his sons to relieve themselves after thousands of years of struggle with the good sausage Python. Philosophies have less value for Dada than an old abandoned toothbrush . . . Dada denounced the infernal ruses of the official vocabulary of wisdom. Dada is for the senseless, which does not mean nonsense. Dada is senseless like nature. Dada is for nature and against art. Dada is direct like nature. Dada is for infinite sense and definite means.'

later to be taken up and systematized, for rather different reasons, by the Surrealists.

For the first couple of years in Zurich Dada was thus still seen, particularly by Ball and Arp, as offering possibilities of a new artistic direction. Ball's desire to restore magic to language, Arp's search for directness in art, can be seen in this way. Ball said: 'The direct and the primitive appear to [the Dadaist] in the midst of this huge anti-nature as being the supernatural itself'. It was even presented publicly in this light; Tzara was to describe the Zurich review *Dada*, when he introduced it to Picabia, as a 'modern art publication'. But with Picabia's arrival in Zurich in August 1918, there was a radical change. The Dadaists had never experienced anyone with such a total disbelief in art, and such an acute sense of the meaninglessness of life. Richter says that meeting him

Jean (Hans) Arp
Forest 1916

Jean (Hans) Arp
Trousse d'un Da 1920

was like an experience of death, and that after such meetings his feelings of despair were so intense that he went round his studio kicking holes in his paintings.

Tzara, the chief impresario and publicist of Zurich Dada, immediately fell under the spell of Picabia's overpowering and magnetic personality; and in his famous *Dada Manifesto 1918* he harnesses his extreme verbal agility to the service of nihilism.

'Philosophy is this question: from which side shall we look at life, God, the idea or other phenomena? Everything one looks at is false. I do not consider the relative result more important than the choice between cake and cherries after dinner. The system of quickly looking at the other side of a thing in order to impose your opinion indirectly is called dialectics, in other words, haggling over the spirit of fried potatoes while dancing method around it.

'If I cry out:

> *Ideal, ideal, ideal,*
> *Knowledge, knowledge, knowledge,*
> *Boomboom, boomboom, boomboom,*

'I have given a pretty faithful version of progress, law, morality and all the other fine qualities that various highly intelligent men have discussed in so many books.'

Dada in Paris

It was Tzara's 1918 Manifesto ('I write a manifesto and I want nothing, yet I say certain things, and in principle I am against manifestos as I am also against principles' that seduced André Breton and other members of the Parisian *Littérature* group. Tzara reached Paris at the very beginning of 1920, and immediately, with the help of Picabia, Breton, the poets Louis Aragon, Philippe Soupault and Georges Ribemont-Dessaignes, and others, set about making the Dada revolt public through outrageous works such as Picabia's *Feathers*. On 23 January the first Dada demonstration took place at the Palais des Fêtes, and as it set the tone for subsequent manifestations it is worth describing in some detail. A talk billed as 'La crise du change' ('The Exchange Crisis') by André Salmon, which had attracted the small shopkeepers of the *quartier* in expectation of financial enlightenment, turned out to be about the overturning of literary values since Symbolism. The audience began to melt away. But Breton's presentation of some Picabia paintings (Picabia never liked to present himself on the stage) began the real event. A large canvas was wheeled on, covered with inscriptions: 'top' at the bottom, 'bottom' at the top, and underneath in large red letters the obscene pun *L.H.O.O.Q. (Elle a chaud au cul)*. As the insult began to sink in, the audience started to shout back at the stage, and with a second 'work' there was uproar. A blackboard appeared, covered with more inscriptions, under the title *Riz au nez*, which Breton immediately rubbed out with a duster. Not only was this not a work of art; it was destroyed before the audience's very eyes. The culmination of the evening was the arrival on stage of Monsieur Dada from Zurich, Tristan Tzara, to present one of his works. He

Das ist das Heil, das sie bringen!

John Heartfield
This is the Salvation They Bring 1938

The Berlin group were critical of Zurich Dada. Huelsenbeck wrote, 'I find in the Dadaism of Tzara and his friends, who made abstract art the cornerstone of their new wisdom, no new idea deserving of very strenuous propaganda. They failed to advance along the abstract road, which ultimately leads from the painted surface to the reality of the post office form.' But the manifesto he and Hausmann drew up, 'What is Dadaism and what it wants in Germany', in its violent swings from rational to extravagant demands, mirrors Dada's uneasy position. '*Dadaism demands*: the international revolutionary union of all creative and intellectual men and women on the basis of radical Communism. . . . The Central Council demands the introduction of the simultaneist poem as a communist state prayer.'

Kurt Schwitters, who operated 'merz', a one-man movement with Dada leanings, in Hanover, tried to join the Berlin group but was rejected. He had, in fact, more in common with those Zurich Dadaists like Arp whom he called 'kernel' Dadaists as opposed to 'husk' Dadaists. The 'kernel' Dadaists include Arp, Picabia, and rather surprisingly, the sculptor Alexandre Archipenko, an indication that the range of Dada sympathizers and friends was much wider than the handful of names usually associated with the movement would lead one to expect. Unembarrassed at calling himself an artist, Schwitters was looking for a renewal of the springs of artistic creation, outside conventional means. He nailed or glued his pictures together from scraps of material, string, wood, bus tickets, chicken-wire and odds and ends he picked up in the street, and then painted them. The result, as in his apparently irrational poems like *Anna Blume*, was an almost lyrical beauty. 'Every artist must be allowed to mould a picture out of nothing but blotting paper, for example, provided he is capable of moulding a picture.'

Dada was a genuinely international event, not just because it operated across political frontiers, but because it consciously attacked patriotic nationalism. Its total effect was far in excess of the energy any individual Dadaist put into it. Each Dadaist brought something different to it and came out with a different idea of what Dada was. The splinters from the bombshell altered the face of art for good.

Kurt Schwitters
Merzpicture 25A, The Star Picture 1920

Kurt Schwitters
Mz 26, 41. okola 1926

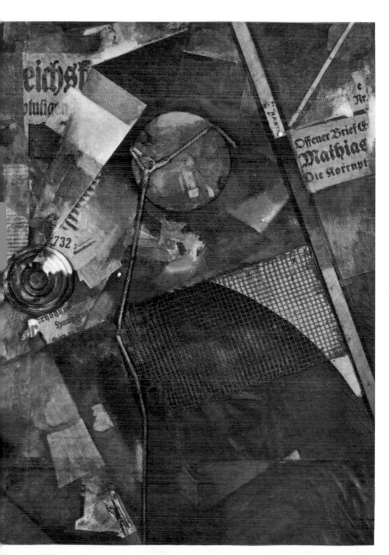

becoming something else. The effect of these drawings on his paintings, hitherto sombre, rather inflexible and heavily influenced by Cubism, was an immediate loosening-up; but working in oil paint he could never achieve the same fluidity. Connected with the automatic drawings were a series of sand paintings he began in 1927. Roughly spreading a canvas with glue, he then sprinkled or threw handfuls of sand on it, tipping the canvas to retain sand only on the glued bits. He then added a few lines or patches of colour, which, as in the drawings, would evoke the image he found there. One of his most radical acts was in the ironically named *Painting*, 1927, where the thick coloured lines have been applied direct from the tube of paint. An exchange between Masson and Matisse in 1932 exemplifies the fundamental difference between Surrealism and other modernist traditions.

André Masson
Painting (Figure) 1927

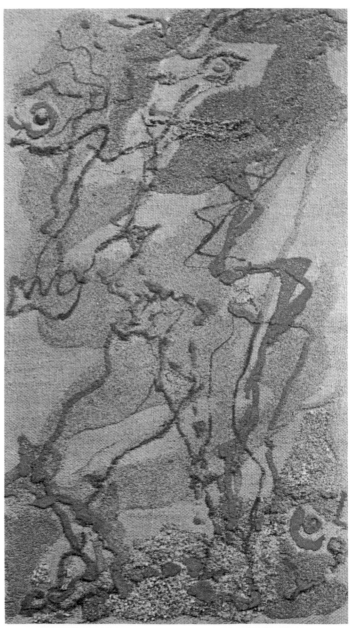

André Masson
Dreamed Embraces 1947

Masson explained: 'I begin without an image or plan in mind, but just draw or paint rapidly according to my impulses. Gradually, in the marks I make, I see suggestions of figures or objects. I encourage these to emerge, trying to bring out their implications even as I now consciously try to give order to the composition.'

'That's curious,' Matisse replied. 'With me it's just the reverse. I always start with something – a chair, a table – but as the work progresses I become less conscious of it. By the end, I am hardly aware of the subject with which I started.'

Whatever the influence certain Surrealist techniques (such as Masson's use of paint direct from the tube) may have had on subsequent abstract artists, such as the Action Painters, the end result for Masson, as for Ernst in his frottages, was fundamentally different, the move being, in Breton's phrase, 'towards the object'.

Max Ernst made his first frottage in 1921, but did not develop the idea any further until 1925, when he took it up as a direct answer to the poets' automatic writing. 'The procedure of frottage, resting thus upon nothing more than the intensification of the irritability of the mind's faculties by appropriate technical means, excluding all conscious mental guidance (of reason, taste, morals), reducing to the extreme the active part of that one

Max Ernst
Head 1925

Max Ernst
Forest and Dove 1927

challenged in 1910 in Italy, where de Chirico was living, by the
Futurists. But while they sought to substitute the beauty of the modern
mechanical world of speed and power, de Chirico painted forgotton
Greek statues, empty, bleached towns. He remembers sitting in a square
in an Italian town staring at a statue, very weak after a long illness, and
suddenly seeing the whole scene in an extraordinarily clear, hallucinatory
light, with an enigmatic intensity which he wanted to reproduce in his
paintings. Sometimes objects appear, disconnected, as though surfacing
from a dream. In *The Song of Love* the green ball, red glove and classical
mask are coupled, like an Ernst collage. The paintings are almost always
empty of human beings, but after a while manikins enter to inhabit the
increasingly stage-like settings.

In 1921–24 Max Ernst did a series of paintings, including *Elephant
Celebes*, *Oedipus Rex* and *Pietà or Revolution by Night*, which are strongly
influenced by de Chirico in their structure and cool intense light as well
as in their actual imagery. They remain very obscure in meaning; if they
are dream images, it is necessary to remember Freud's warning, when he
was asked to contribute to a Surrealist anthology of dreams: 'a mere
collection of dreams, without the dreamer's associations, without

Giorgio de Chirico
Conquest of the Philosopher 1912

Giorgio de Chirico
The Song of Love 1914

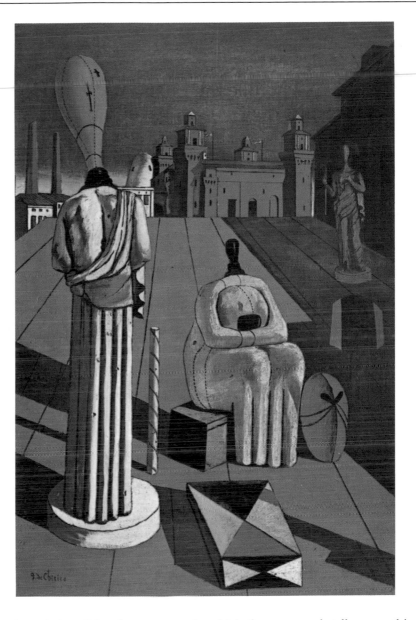

Giorgio de Chirico
Disquieting Muses 1917

knowledge of the circumstances in which they occurred, tells me nothing, and I can hardly imagine what it would tell anyone.'

Wary of psychoanalysis in the absence of the conditions required by Freud, we may still suggest, in *Oedipus Rex*, bearing in mind Ernst's frequent and ambiguous references to his father, that the Oedipus legend as interpreted by Freud, whom Ernst had read, bore a personal significance for him. Oedipus blinded himself, and the references to eyes in the painting are disturbingly underlined by the balloon behind, a quotation from Odilon Redon's *The Eye like a Strange Balloon*.

Ernst shared the Surrealists' taste for exotic and primitive art. In *Elephant Celebes* the elephant itself is based on a photograph of an African

Of the other makers of the 'hand-painted dream picture', the former Dadaist Man Ray produced perhaps the most spectacular images, such as *Observatory Time – The Lovers*. Victor Brauner's paintings, such as *The Philosopher's Stone*, are metamorphoses, evoking magical icons. In the work of Pierre Roy, and above all in that of René Magritte, the image is fixed in a flat, dead paint surface.

Some Magritte paintings may really be memories of dreams. *The Lovers*, with their heads swathed in cloth, could be a dream transformation of his terrible memories of his mother's death, when he was a child; she was found drowned with her white gown wrapped round her head. It is impossible to know. But most of his paintings take the form of a dialogue with the world, a questioning of the reality of real phenomena, and their relation with their painted image (*The Human Condition*). Sometimes by disruption of the scale of objects he can turn something harmless into something menacing (like the monstrous Alice-through-the-looking-glass apple in *The Listening Room*) or puzzling (*Personal Values*). Often, although the image exists – there it is in the painting – it is impossible to grasp it because it is beyond our logical understanding: in *The Field-Glass* an open window reveals blackness beyond. Clouds are reflected in the shut casement, but the other casement is open, revealing an empty frame. *On the Threshold of Liberty* is a room panelled with motifs from Magritte's own paintings, with a cannon threatening violence or rape. His cover for a Surrealist magazine is perhaps his frankest expression of the violence underlying Surrealist imagery.

In 1949 Magritte wrote a manifesto, *Le Vrai Art de la peinture* (which incidentally contains an attack on the 'magnetic fields of chance', an allusion to Breton and Soupault's early work), to explain his idea of the true function of painting, as opposed to its real rival, the cinema. 'The art

Man Ray
Observatory Time – The Lovers 1932–34

Right, above:

René Magritte
On the Threshold of Liberty 1929

René Magritte
Personal Values 1952

Right, below:

René Magritte
Cover of *Minotaure*, no. 10, 1937

René Magritte
The Human Condition I 1933

MINOTAURE

First, one must remember that the dream for Freud, and also for
Breton, was a direct path to the unconscious; the way in which a dream
deals with its subject, condensing, distorting, allowing contradictory facts
or impressions to exist side by side without any conflict – what Freud calls
dream-work – is characteristic of the processes of the unconscious. The
manifest content of the dream, what we remember when we wake up,
probably masks latent, hidden meanings, which may be revealed by the
dreamer's associations, achieved through analysis. For most of the
Surrealists dreams were valuable simply for their poetic content, as
documents from a marvellous world, whose hidden sexual symbolism
none the less filled them with delight. The first number of the Surrealist
periodical *La Révolution surréaliste* contained simple accounts of dreams by
Breton, De Chirico, Renée Gauthier; 'Only the dream leaves man with
all his rights to liberty.' Dali, on the other hand, especially in the late
1920s and early 1930s, presents dream images whose content is made

Salvador Dali
The Dismal Sport 1929

Salvador Dali
Giraffe in Flames 1935

Salvador Dali
Impressions of Africa 1938

manifest. Freud, who met Dali, and found him infinitely more interesting
than the other Surrealists, immediately understood what Dali was doing.
'It is not the unconscious I seek in your pictures, but the conscious. While
in the pictures of the masters – Leonardo or Ingres – that which interests
me, that which seems mysterious and troubling to me, is precisely the
search for unconscious ideas, of an enigmatic order, hidden in the picture.
Your mystery is manifested outright. The picture is but a mechanism to
reveal itself.' Dali had read Freud, as well as Krafft-Ebing on the
psychopathology of sex, and his 'vice of self-interpretation, not only of my
dreams but of everything that happened to me, however accidental it
might seem at first glance', is clear not only in his paintings but in books
like *Le Mythe tragique de l'Angélus de Millet*, in which the hidden content of
Millet's painting, and hence the cause of Dali's obsession with it, reveals
itself to him through a series of associations, coincidences and dreams.

The Dismal Sport (*Le Jeu lugubre*), a painting which made the Surrealists
hesitate before admitting Dali to their group, fearing it revealed
coprophiliac tendencies in Dali, swarms (as does *Illumined Pleasures*) with
examples of symbols straight from the pages of text-books of psychoanalysis. It is impossible to tell what may be a dream image, and what
Dali's analysis of it. Certainly the images make perfectly clear Dali's fear
of sex, guilt about masturbatory fantasies, and consequent castration
fears. In another series of paintings Dali interprets the legend of William
Tell as a kind of reversed Oedipal myth about castration. Like *The Dismal
Sport*, the *Giraffe in Flames* bunches its matter into concentrated areas of
canvas, a deliberate analogy with Freud's description of dream-work.

'The only difference between myself and a madman is that I am not
mad,' Dali once said. He turned his willed paranoia into a system that he

6 Abstract Expressionism

ANTHONY EVERITT

The social and political upheavals of the Depression and the disruption caused by the war against Hitler had a profound effect on young artists in Europe and America. Technological advances no longer seemed a guarantee of social or political progress. The hopeful rationalism of modern society was discredited. As far as art was concerned, the logical, idealistic premises of Cubism and the movements which flowed from it in the years between the two wars had lost their appeal.

The generation which began to paint in the 1930s and early 1940s was in a desperate frame of mind. A new approach was urgently needed to resolve what was seen as a crisis of subject matter. 'The situation was so bad that I know I felt free to try anything, no matter how absurd it seemed,' the American painter Adolph Gottlieb observed. He and many of his contemporaries were tentatively moving towards an aesthetic which repudiated the hegemony of intellect and allowed the artist to express himself freely and subjectively. As another American, Robert Motherwell, put it: 'The need is for felt experience – intense, immediate, direct, subtle, unified, warm, vivid, rhythmic.'

Many painters began to concentrate on the act of painting itself, unimpeded by anything save the decision to paint. Their thinking rested on an already well-established principle. If they emptied their minds of preconceptions, and applied pigment with a maximum of spontaneity, the images they made would be an expression of the deepest levels of their being. Everybody was agreed that this was a worthy objective: modern depth psychology appeared to show that the conscious mind could exert a repressive authority on the unconscious, and that, if it released its hold, the springs of feelings would flow clear again. Art, then, became a method of self-realization.

The Surrealists had shown the way. Taking their cue from the procedures of psychoanalysis – especially free association – they formulated the technique of automatism, according to which the painter or writer operated, metaphorically speaking, blindfold. He welcomed accident and exploited the random, doing anything in fact that would send the ego to sleep. André Breton's original definition of Surrealism, given in the First Manifesto of 1924, still held good: 'SURREALISM, noun. Pure psychic automatism by which it is intended to express, either verbally or in writing [he soon enlarged this definition to include visual art], the true function of thought. Thought dictated in the absence of all control exerted by reason, and outside all aesthetic or moral preoccupations.'

Mark Rothko
No. 61 1953

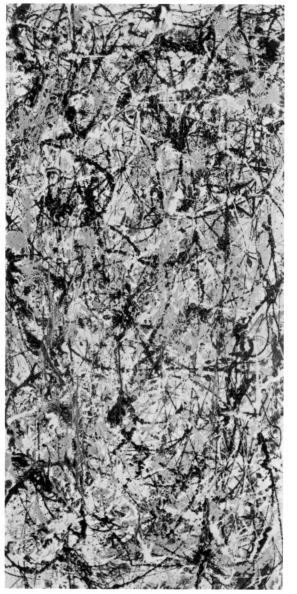

represented a commitment to emotional honesty. Robert Motherwell
wrote in 1950: 'The process of painting then is conceived of as an
adventure, without preconceived ideas, on the part of persons of
intelligence, sensibility and passion. Fidelity to what occurs between
oneself and the canvas, no matter how unexpected, becomes central. . . .
The major decisions in the process of painting are on the grounds of
truth, not taste. . . . No artist ends up with the style he expected to have
when he began.'

Willem De Kooning shared the leadership of the New York gestural
avant-garde with Pollock. However, he remained on far closer terms with
his aesthetic antecedents than did many of his peers. The movement
which specially attracted him was Cubism; but his general attachment to
tradition can also be seen in his acceptance of the human figure as a
suitable subject for painting.

Jackson Pollock
Cathedral 1947

Jackson Pollock
Easter and the Totem 1953

Born in Rotterdam in 1904, he spent his first twenty-one years in Europe and studied in Antwerp, Brussels and Rotterdam. He moved to the United States in 1926, but only started to paint full-time when he found employment with the Federal Art Project. In his early work he painfully came to grips with the problem of treating three-dimensional figures without upsetting the integrity of the picture surface. In works of the early to middle 1940s, from the *Seated Woman* of 1940 to the *Pink Angel* of 1947, his solution was to play down modelling and, gradually, to isolate individual parts of the human body and treat them as planes. Painterly silhouettes, suggesting household objects and also biomorphic forms (he was a close friend of Arshile Gorky), are crowded together on a plain ground; there is little sense of space, of *in front* or *behind*, and the images and the gaps between them become to some extent interchangeable.

After 1942, De Kooning experimented with automatism, which loosened his handling of paint and encouraged him to exploit the ambiguity of semi-abstract signs. It also introduced a new vehemence in his brushwork. All this laid the ground for his sudden adoption in 1947 of a new style in a series of black and white pictures in household enamel

Willem De Kooning
Seated Woman c. 1940

Willem De Kooning
Pink Angel c. 1947

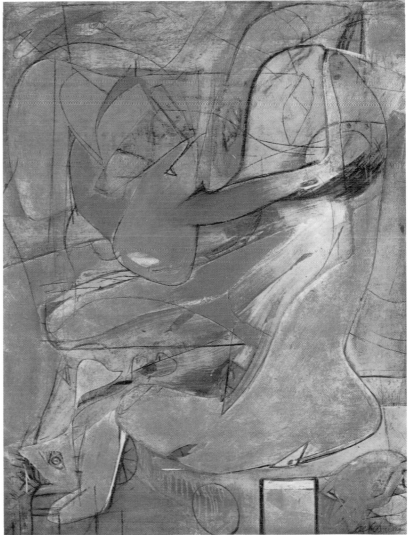

and Cornell University. He taught during the 1930s, and did not participate in the Federal Art Project: 'I paid a severe price for not being on the project with the other guys; in their eyes I wasn't a painter; I didn't have a label.' During the 1930s he was attracted by left-wing thinking, and he has been quoted as saying: 'My politics went towards open forms and free situations; I was a very vocal anarchist.'

Newman was an important polemicist, and passed through all the phases of Abstract Expressionism. In 1947, with Rothko, Motherwell and Baziotes, he helped to found a school called 'Subjects of the Artist' and to edit *Tiger's Eye*, a magazine which argued the case for an aesthetic based on myth. Although he rebelled against academic Surrealism, Newman explored automatist procedures. The archetypal forms and plastic energy of the North-West Coast Indians impressed him, as did pre-Columbian art; 'My idea was that, with an automatic move, you could create a world.'

Barnett Newman
Untitled 1945

Barnett Newman
Onement I 1948

Barnett Newman
Achilles 1952

Something of what he meant appears in *Untitled* (1945); the gesture creates a world in which biomorphs and a prophetic road-like band cross a remote, creamy cosmic space. By 1948 Newman was ready to abandon subject matter, whether abstract or figurative. *Onement I*, painted in that year, marks the turning point in his style. A thickly painted vertical strip lies just off-centre over masking tape. No doubt Newman had intended quite another picture; and, as Charles Harrison points out, the refusal to lift the tape or to 'paint up' the ground were long-meditated decisions.

The picture prefigures the basic features of his later work. A repudiation of sensuously handled paint goes hand in hand with the disappearance of 'form' – that is, of pictorial elements and of design. The canvas becomes an undifferentiated field which is defined rather than divided by the stripe (or, as in *Vir Heroicus Sublimis*, painted in 1950–51, stripes). These thin bands neutrally echo the boundaries of the picture plane, and read like a serial sequence which could be repeated indefinitely beyond them.

But for all its importance, drawing is subordinate to colour. In *Vir Heroicus Sublimis* and in *Achilles* of 1952, the great expanse of red subdues the ego and inspires a kind of tranquil awe. The non-painterliness of Newman's technique, however, prevents the spectator from indulging himself in sensation. By its dryness and banality, it draws attention away from the experience towards the idea.

Mark Rothko's soft, luminous palette is more sensuous than Newman's. Veils of thin pigment wash over the canvas and soak into it; warm colour lies over cool, cool over warm, dark over light, and light over dark. But sensuousness is not the same as hedonism. Rothko's colour fields have a contemplative intensity and invite a surrender of self. Among the ingredients of his art he listed: 'A clear preoccupation with death. All art deals with intimations of mortality.'

Born in Russia in 1903, Rothko emigrated with his family to the United States at the age of ten, in 1913. Between 1921 and 1923 he studied at Yale University and attended Max Weber's drawing classes at the Art Students' League. In 1935 he was co-founder of the Ten, a group of Expressionistic artists who opposed the post-Cubist abstraction represented by American Abstract Artists. Before the war he painted human figures in deserted cityscapes.

In the early 1940s, like many of his contemporaries, he experimented with automatism and Jungian biomorphism. He painted amalgams of human, plant, animal and fish forms. His figures are arranged schematically against soft light-filled grounds (*Entombment I*, 1946). They express, as Rothko said of an early painting in this manner, 'a pantheism in which man, bird, beast and tree – the known as well as the unknowable – merge into a single tragic idea.'

Around 1947, that *annus mirabilis* of the New York School, Rothko exchanged his linear emblems for soft-focus blurs of colour, eventually reducing them to two or three roughly rectangular shapes stacked one on top of the other. At the same time he increased the size of his canvases and started to work on a monumental scale.

Although Rothko's compositions can be broken down into separate components, he found ways of preserving the integrity of the 'field'. There

Mark Rothko
Black on Grey 1970

Mark Rothko
Red, White and Brown 1957

is no central point of attention. His rectangles fill the picture, the shape of which they repeat and confirm. Because of his use of wash the unifying texture of the canvas shows through. With a touch of irony, he encourages a contradiction between the illusion of a cloudy depth and the hard, visible fact of a surface.

The atmosphere of mature works such as *Red, White and Brown* of 1957 is passive and meditative. Opaque mists of disembodied colour invite the spectator into a quiet space, metaphorically equivalent to reverie. They express a not displeasing melancholy, close in feeling to Vergil's *sunt lacrimae rerum et mentem mortalia tangunt*: 'There are tears in the nature of things, and hearts are touched by transience.'

Rothko did not change this stylistic formula, but his colours gradually darkened. Late canvases such as *Black on Grey* are bleakly pessimistic. His life ended in suicide in 1970.

Adolph Gottlieb's development followed the same pattern as Rothko's: mythic figuration yielded to abstract emblems on a blank ground. However, he did not go so fast or so far. Born in 1903 in New York, he trained at the Art Students' League, travelled through Europe and spent some time in Paris. During the 1930s he painted realistic views of the American scene. Under the impact of Surrealism and Freudian psychology, as well as Klee and Mondrian, Gottlieb devised a personal manner based on an irregular grid, containing images drawn from primitive art and parts of the human anatomy, for paintings which he called *Pictographs*. He adopted this name because 'it was necessary for me to utterly repudiate so called "good painting" in order to express what was visually true for me'. Curiously, as his career progressed, he appears to have become increasingly concerned with technique. His pictures are tidy and personable and present themselves to their best advantage.

In the early 1950s, after a decade of *Pictographs*, Gottlieb rationalized his principles of composition: as in *Frozen Sounds No. 1*, an earth-like band stretches across the lower part of the canvas, and in a pale 'sky' above hangs a row of ovoid or rectangular discs. Further reduction followed in 1957 with his *Burst* series. A single 'sun' now dominates the top half of the picture: it has a passivity which is in sharp contrast to the active linearity of the interlaced bundle of brush-strokes below. Gottlieb's observations on Gorky some years previously are a good description of his own *Bursts*: 'What he felt, I suppose, was a sense of polarity, not of dichotomy: that opposites could exist simultaneously within a body, within a painting or within an entire art.'

In a picture like *Brink*, painted in 1959, Gottlieb has nearly arrived at a colour field position. But his discs and exploding patches remain anecdotal incidents; he was willing to generalize and abstract the 'pictograph' or sign, but he refused to banish it altogether, whether by elimination (Newman) or magnification (Rothko). Cautious and consistent, Gottlieb stayed within what he knew until his death in 1974.

Adolph Gottlieb
Brink 1959

Adolph Gottlieb
The Frozen Sounds Number 1 1951

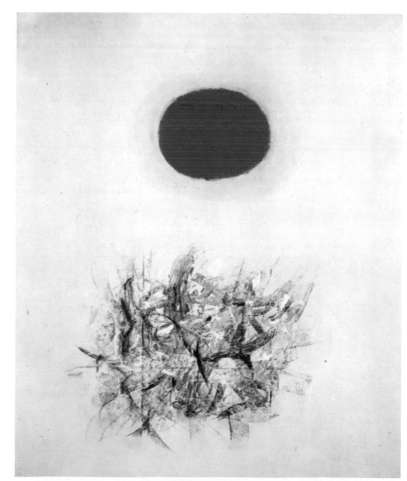

Clyfford Still is an artist of a more uncompromising frame of mind. His attitude to the avant-garde was as dismissive as that of Pollock's teacher, Benton; and, having passed through Bauhaus, Dada, Surrealist and Cubist phases, Still then obdurately turned his back on contemporary art movements. 'That ultimate in irony – the Armory Show of 1913 – had dumped on us the combined and sterile conclusions of European decadence,' was his final conclusion. In its place he cultivated a pioneering individualism – an attitude which, in its way, is as American as apple-pie. Art was a way of life, a matter of conscience: 'Hell, it's not just about painting – any fool can put colour on canvas.'

Still, born in North Dakota in 1904, studied at Spokane and Washington State universities, obtaining a master's degree in 1935, and spent six years as a teacher. The representational work he did during these years anticipates his later abstractions: a vertical figure stands in an open landscape, and there is a moral duality symbolized in sun and earth, light and dark.

Still moved to an early 'myth-making' manner which resembled that of Rothko and Gottlieb, although arrived at independently. In 1941 his artistic production was curtailed by war work; after a one-man show in San Francisco in 1943 he resumed full-time painting, and during the next few years he abandoned figuration for good. He did so with a characteristic decisiveness, saying later: 'I have no brief for signs or symbols or literary allusions in painting. They are crutches for illustrators and politicians desperate for an audience.'

Clyfford Still
Painting 1948–D 1948

Clyfford Still
1951 Yellow 1951

Clyfford Still
Painting 1958

Clyfford Still
Painting 1951

Still devised a distinctive format to which he has since kept. *Painting 1948-D, 1951 Yellow*, and *Painting 1951* show a colour field corroded by torn flame-like verticals. Still's designs are rationally organized and are, as Lawrence Alloway has observed, 'like the colour code of a map . . . that is turning back into a substantial reality; not a key to somewhere else, but itself a land'.

Although this is a useful metaphor, the reference to landscape should not be taken too literally. 'The fact that I grew up on the prairies has nothing to do with my paintings, with what people think they find in them,' Still said in an interview. 'I paint only myself, not nature.'

During the 1940s he reduced his originally brilliant chromaticism: his fields became black or opaque purple. Forms or pictorial disturbances which had occurred in the centre of the picture are pushed to the sides. Then, in the 1950s, an unexpected lyricism makes an appearance, and in works like *Painting 1958* colours seem more content to please than previously.

Still, like Newman, has an exalted notion of art. His aim is to purify the act of painting so that it can transcend itself and become a self-sufficient assertion of the sublime. He once compared the artist to a man who journeys through a wasted terrain and reaches a high plateau: 'Imagination, no longer fettered by the laws of fear, became as one with Vision. And the Act, intrinsic and absolute, was its meaning, and the bearer of its passion.'

'forming with colour', and his interest, both pedagogic and creative, lay in finding a synthesis of Cubist structure and a Fauvist palette. (Clement Greenberg claimed that 'you could learn more about Matisse's colour [from Hofmann] than from Matisse himself'.)

Hofmann painted in a semi-abstract manner between 1936 and 1941; his subjects were always identifiable and were organized in brightly coloured, structured areas. From 1942 he swam with the tide, practising automatism and devising a biomorphic vocabulary of forms. He also invented an original drip and splash technique (anticipating Pollock).

In 1946 Hofmann began the series of abstractions for which he is best remembered. *Transfiguration*, of 1947, for instance, consists of energetically painted areas with some linear elements. Traces of Cubist organization remain, but the design is held in balance by the 'push and pull' interaction between three-dimensional depth and two-dimensional surface. 'Every movement releases a counter-movement,' he wrote. 'A represented form that does not owe its existence to a perception of movement is not a form.' In the 1950s Hofmann experimented with many different modes of expression. In some canvases, such as *Fantasia in Blue*, rectangles overloaded with richly coloured pigment are placed among free gestural areas, and in others, towards 1960 and after, such as *Rising Moon*, broad semi-transparent washes glow from a white ground.

Robert Motherwell is another New York artist with a distinctively European bent. Born in 1915, he entered Stanford University and later

Hans Hofmann
Fantasia in Blue 1954

Hans Hofmann
Rising Moon 1964

Harvard, where he studied art history. He took a somewhat dilettante view of culture and the good life, and lamented the disappearance of 'the wonderful things of the past – the late afternoon encounters, the leisurely repasts, the discriminations of taste, the graces of manners, and the gratuitous cultivation of minds'.

In 1940 he met the Surrealists-in-exile, and, as well as introducing him to automatism and Freudian psychology, they confirmed his instinct for nineteenth-century French aesthetics. Leaning on Baudelaire's theory of correspondences, according to which 'scents, colours and sounds respond to one another', Motherwell held that complete abstraction was impossible: 'The "pure" red of which certain abstractionists speak does not exist. Any red is rooted in blood, glass, wine, hunter's caps and a thousand other concrete phenomena.'

Motherwell experimented with collage, and his early works are influenced by Picasso, Matisse and Schwitters; but his first major paintings, the series entitled *Elegies to the Spanish Republic*, were begun in 1949 (by 1965, he had finished more than a hundred). Vertical rectangles and ovals spread across these long frieze-like canvases. The colouring is usually black on white. According to Motherwell, 'the pictures are . . . general metaphors for life and death, and their interrelation'. This

Robert Motherwell
Je t'aime, II A 1955

compositions are made up from a lattice of broad black bands, like the enlarged strokes of a housepainter's brush. Born in 1919 in France, his early interests were in prehistoric and Romanesque art. He was impressed by exhibitions of Cézanne and Picasso which he saw in 1938–39. After 1946 he began to exhibit in Paris. Although, like many of his contemporaries, Soulages was attracted to gesture, to the wide sweep of the arm across the canvas, this was more for the architectonic possibilities which it offered than for the excitement of movement. His pictures, of which *Painting* (1959) is a characteristic example, follow a rational programme: a framework of black bands is painted on a more or less plain, brightly coloured ground, and this, in turn, is overlaid with folding vertical or diagonal bands. The result is a gravely monumental structure: the upper levels set up dynamic formal and spatial rhythms, but these are firmly contained within the lower ones. Such formality contrasts with the more spontaneous gestures of, say, Kline's *King Oliver* (1958). Soulages was firm in his commitment to abstraction itself: 'I do not start from an

Pierre Soulages
Painting 1959

Georges Mathieu
Mathieu from Alsace goes to Ramsey Abbey

object or from a landscape with a view to distorting them, nor, conversely, do I seek, as I paint, to provoke their appearance.' (Compare, again, Kline's easy-going attitude, p. 281).

Georges Mathieu, born in 1921, was one of the earliest Frenchmen to appreciate the significance of the New York School, and has been a tireless propagandist for what he refers to as Lyrical Abstraction. He admires the art of the age of Louis XIV, and seems to have seen his role as that of an arbiter of taste, a contemporary Le Brun. A great organizer of exhibitions and publisher of manifestos, usually formulated in high rhetorical terms, he began to paint in 1942, under the Surrealist influence of Matta and Masson. Deeply moved by paintings of Wols which he saw in 1947, he soon developed his own personal style. Both in principle and in practice he was close to the Abstract Expressionists. He talked of 'the intrinsic autonomy of the work of art', and of the 'phenomenology of the "very act of painting"'.

Mathieu believes that conscious intention is best expelled from painting by an extreme rapidity of execution. He has painted in public on a number of occasions, and in Tokyo he once completed a canvas over twelve metres long in less than twenty minutes. However, except for some early works, his pictures are more decorative than aggressive: as in *Mathieu from Alsace . . .,* laceries of bright pigment (red, white, black and blue are his favourite colours) stretch horizontally across the middle of the pictures or spread out from a central coagulation of pigment like overpainted Chinese characters. Because they keep a good distance from the edges of the canvas, they do not function as an all-over field. Mathieu's work has an appealing *joie de vivre*, although his real achievement lies in the field of publicity.

Henry Michaux, born in Belgium in 1899, moved freely throughout his life between literature and visual art. His preferred medium was ink on

Henri Michaux
Painting in India Ink 1966

paper, and painting was for him a non-verbal extension of writing – a carrying on of poetry by other means. Like Hartung and Mathieu, he was influenced by Oriental calligraphy; and he spoke of being 'possessed by movements, completely tensed by these forms which came at me full speed, in rhythmic succession'. This is a good summary of his drawing technique; blots (*taches*) pour on to the paper in quick succession, under the pressure of emotion and, on occasion, mescalin. As in *Painting in India Ink*, of 1966, these blots come together into a so-called field of energy, which the eye can read, passing from one small expressive sign to another.

A host of subsidiary figures complicate the post-war Parisian art scene. Many had been working in figurative styles in the 1930s, and their early concerns informed their later manners. Jean Bazaine, born in 1904, moved in his forties from a representational post-Cubist position towards a free abstraction inspired by nature, as in *Child and the Night* (1949). An original feature of his work is that his compositions seem to pour over the edge of the canvas and so subvert its arbitrary rectangularity. Alfred Manessier, born in 1911, has followed much the same course as Bazaine, ending up with a symbolic, landscaped-based abstraction which expresses a mystical Christian viewpoint; a typical title is *Night in Gethsemane*. His

Jean Bazaine
Child and the Night 1949

Alfred Manessier
Night in Gethsemane 1952

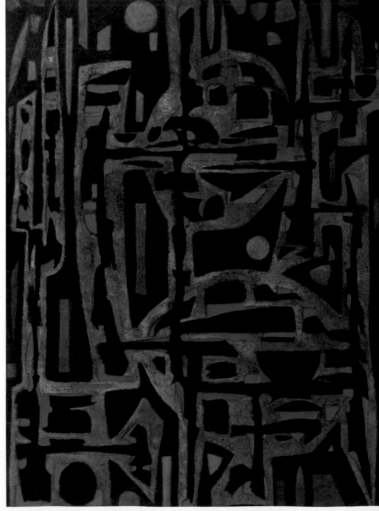

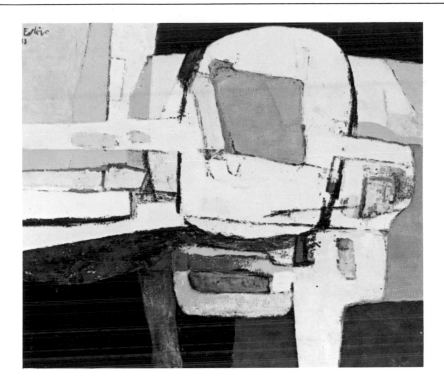

Maurice Estève
Friselune 1958

finest work is in stained glass. Maurice Estève, born in 1904, passed
through most phases of modern art before devising his own variant of free
abstraction, in which painterly but static compositions are assembled and
unified by a rich palette. Although he has been defined as a colourist, a
work like *Friselune* (1958) also has a constructed planar quality deriving
from Cézanne.

Nicolas de Staël was born in St Petersburg in 1914 and lived mostly in
Belgium and France until his suicide in 1955. By his economical
illusionism and his decorative palette, De Staël achieved considerable
popularity. But he was never a painter's painter, and made
comparatively little impression on his contemporaries or successors. His
career is of interest because it reflects an unwillingness to make a
complete commitment either to abstraction or to figuration. Not unlike
the *Nocturnes* of Whistler, his vividly coloured designs read equally well as
harmonious arrangements of pure form or as stylized but atmospheric
evocations of landscape. In one respect the tables are turned: his titles,
unlike Whistler's, suggest representation (*Figure by the Sea*, 1952).
Ambivalence permeated De Staël's whole aesthetic approach: 'For myself,
in order to develop, I need always to function differently, from one thing
to another, without an *a priori* aesthetic. I lose contact with the canvas
every moment and find it again and lose it. This is absolutely necessary,
because I believe in accident – as soon as I feel too logical, this upsets me
and I turn naturally to illogicality.'

The Surrealists and German Expressionists attracted a following in the
smaller countries of Northern Europe. In the late 1930s some Danes
harnessed automatism and a painterly manner to their national folklore,

Nicolas de Staël
Figure by the Sea 1952

filling their canvases with the trolls, gods and dragons of Nordic mythology. This runic Expressionism was offered as a corrective to 'sterile abstraction'. It drew some support from painters in Belgium and Holland. The movement was institutionalized when in 1948 a group of Danish, Belgian and Dutch artists in Paris formed 'Cobra' (named from the first letters of Copenhagen, Brussels and Amsterdam). They included Karel Appel, Constant, Corneille, Christian Dotremont, Asger Jorn and Philippe Noiret; they were joined later by Atlan, Pierre Alechinsky and the Germans Karl Otto Götz and Otto Piene.

A keynote of Cobra was a high-spirited violence both in terms of style and content. In the aftermath of war, its members saw themselves as resistance fighters for art. They delighted in expressive exaggeration: 'It is snowing colours,' said Dotremont. 'The colours are like a scream.'

The dominant figure was Asger Jorn, born in Jutland in 1911. With a background of automatist Surrealism, he saw the artist, in familiar terms, as a heroic individualist, and painting as an existential gesture: 'Art is the unique act of man or the unique in human actions.' Kandinsky, Miró

Asger Jorn
Unlimited 1959–60

and Klee influenced his work; but Le Corbusier and Léger also impressed
him by their rigorous simplifications. A linear technique slowly gave way
to a savage painterliness, and at the height of his powers in the second
half of the 1950s, Jorn applied pigment in broad bands and blotches of
luminous colour (*Unlimited*, 1959–60). He never altogether abandoned his
obsession with myth, and the hallucinatory images of legend lurk within
his disturbed, swirling compositions.

Corneille, born Cornelis van Beverloo in Belgium in 1922, studied
drawing in Amsterdam. His inspiration is drawn from landscape, and his
Informal Abstractionist paintings are tranquil and cheerful, especially in
comparison with his excitable colleagues. His early work is indebted to

7 *Pop*

SIMON WILSON

The term 'Pop art' refers to a stylistic development in Western art which occurred roughly between 1956 and 1966 in Great Britain and the United States. There were related developments in Europe during the same period.

Pop art has three major distinguishing characteristics. Firstly, it is both figurative and realist, something that avant-garde art had not been since its very beginnings with Courbet's Realism. In 1861 Courbet published a manifesto of Realism in the Paris *Courrier du dimanche* in which he stated that for an artist the practice of art should involve 'bringing to bear his faculties on the ideas and objects of the period in which he lives'. Six years earlier he had stated the same thing in more personal terms in the short manifesto attached to the catalogue of his 1855 exhibition: 'To know in order to be able to do, that was my thought. To be in a position to translate the habits, the ideas, the appearance of my time . . . in a word, to make a living art, that is my aim.' This vitally important idea that artists must deal with the contemporary world and with life as well as with art is also the basis of Pop art. Just over a century after Courbet's manifesto, Roy Lichtenstein, one of the creators of Pop art in America, told an interviewer: 'Outside is the world; it's there. Pop art looks out into the world.'

Secondly, Pop was created in New York and London, and the world it looks out on is therefore the very special world of the great mid-twentieth-century metropolis. Pop is rooted in the urban environment. Not only that, but Pop looks at special aspects of that environment, aspects which because of their associations and cultural level seemed at first impossible as subjects of art. These were: comics and picture magazines; advertisements and packaging of all kinds; the world of popular entertainment, including Hollywood movies, pop music and fairgrounds, amusement arcades, radio, television and tabloid newspapers; consumer durables, especially perhaps refrigerators and automobiles; highways and gas stations; foodstuffs, especially hot dogs, ice cream and pie; and, last but not least, money.

Thirdly, Pop artists deal with this subject matter in a very special way. On one hand they insist that the comic strip or soup can or whatever is simply a 'motif', an excuse for a painting, like an apple in a still-life by Cézanne. Roy Lichtenstein, for example has stated: 'Once I am involved with the painting I think of it as an abstraction. Half the time they are upside down anyway when I work.' On the other hand, whereas in a Cézanne the motif is a traditional and familiar one, and it is easy for the

Andy Warhol
Shot Light Blue Marilyn 1964

spectator to ignore it and concentrate on the formal qualities of the
painting, in Pop art the motif is in no way traditional, is of a kind which
had never before been used as a basis for art, and therefore strongly
engages the spectator's attention.

Not only was the motif of a new kind; its presentation was often
(especially in the work of Roy Lichtenstein and Andy Warhol) startlingly
literal – it looked more like the real thing than ever before in the history
of art. The result was a kind of art which combined the abstract and the
figurative in a quite new way: it was realism, but done in the light and
full knowledge of all that had happened in modern art since the time of
Courbet.

New York

Marcel Duchamp arrived in New York from Paris in 1915. With him he
brought, as a present for his friend, the collector Walter Arensberg, one of
his own works, a part of Paris (some of its air, in fact) simply enclosed in
a glass globe. Duchamp had begun to produce works of this type, called
'readymades', two years before in 1913. They were bits of reality –
usually man-made objects, but sometimes, as with *Paris Air*, taken from
nature – presented as art, either modified ('assisted') or with no more
intervention by the artist than an inscription or just a signature. The first
'assisted readymade' was the 1913 *Bicycle Wheel* (*see* pp. 204–06), and it
was in New York in 1917 that he produced his most notorious
readymade, the *Fountain*, a men's urinal of the wall-mounted type which
Duchamp simply signed R. Mutt (apparently the name of a sanitary
engineer). These works were not intended as sensuous objects but as
demonstrations of an idea. The assisted readymades illustrate the
proposition that the work of an artist – any artist – consists essentially in
the assembling of pre-existent materials, which may perfectly well be

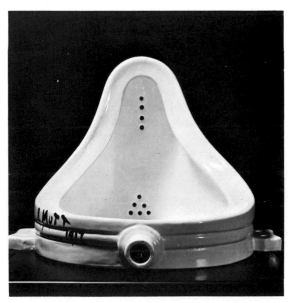

Marcel Duchamp
Fountain 1917

readymade ones. The readymades proper go even further in showing that the creating of art need not necessarily be a manual activity but can be purely a matter of making choices. They also showed that no aspect of the world could be considered to lie outside the artist's scope. These were the ideas that were taken up again in New York (where Duchamp was still living and working) by Robert Rauschenberg and Jasper Johns, and passed on by them to the Pop artists.

In 1955 Rauschenberg made his painting *Bed*, consisting of real bedclothes with paint slurped and dripped over them, the whole then mounted and hung on the wall. This was one of the first of his so-called combine paintings, in which the paint is used to integrate real objects into the work. These paintings, often intruded parts of themselves into the

Robert Rauschenberg
Bed 1955

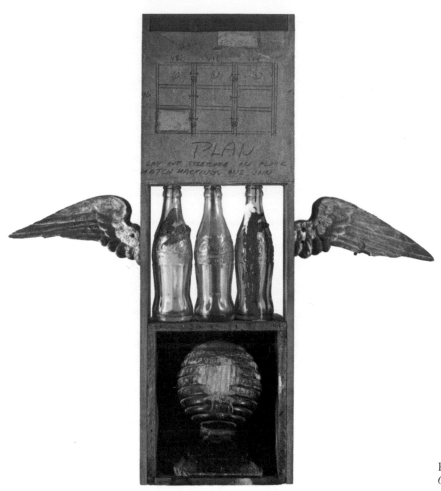

Robert Rauschenberg
Coca-Cola Plan 1958

spectator's space – i.e. they became part of the real world – and it was at
the time he was making them that Rauschenberg also made his
significant and much-quoted remark that he was operating 'in the gap
between art and life'. As well as the combine paintings Rauschenberg
made fully three-dimensional works, one of which, *Coca-Cola Plan* of 1958,
prominently incorporated three Coca-Cola bottles, objects which were
later to become one of the major motifs of Pop art.

   Like Rauschenberg, Jasper Johns is both a painter and a constructor of
objects, and his contribution to the development of Pop art was, if
anything, more significant than that of his fellow artist. Also from about
1955, Johns began to produce extraordinary paintings of familiar, even
banal, objects and images, initially targets and the American flag,
although later he used maps of the USA and numbers. These motifs
possessed three vital qualities for Johns: they were very familiar; they
were two-dimensional; and they were simple and visually striking.
Depicting a two-dimensional object like the American flag in the two-
dimensional medium of painting resulted in works which were at a casual

Jasper Johns
US Flag 1958

glance indistinguishable from the real thing, an effect Johns strongly
reinforced in some of his flag paintings by taking the flag right to the edge
of the canvas and eliminating any illusion of it being an image on a
ground. At the same time the flag is a bold abstract design, and Johns's
paintings of it are executed in a range of ravishing colours (sometimes
close to the original, sometimes not), in a technique of extreme painterly
refinement and sensuousness, so that they mark the first appearance in
American painting of that combination of strong formal and abstract
qualities with familiar, immediately recognizable imagery which is a
characteristic of Pop art.

Johns applied the same system in three-dimensional art when he made
his famous sculpture of two Ballantyne Ale cans in 1960. More perhaps
than the flag paintings, these beer cans looks so close to their source as

Jasper Johns
Ale Cans 1964

almost to preclude the possibility of their being art. But in fact they are beautifully cast in patinated bronze; the labels are meticulously hand-painted; and, thus translated, the twin cylinders assert a strongly sculptural quality.

The new possibilities offered by the art of Johns and Rauschenberg were taken up by the Pop artists in New York partly in reaction against the dominance of Abstract Expressionism. This kind of painting was based on the idea that art should be a direct record of the artist's inner impulses and states of mind, and it was therefore intensely personal and unworldly – precisely the opposite of Pop art, in fact. It manifested itself in a variety of forms, between the two extremes of Jackson Pollock's dynamic, gestural action painting and Mark Rothko's static, softly brushed fields of colour. It was Roy Lichtenstein who best articulated the Pop artists' attitude to Abstract Expressionism when he said: 'art has become extremely romantic and unrealistic, feeding on art, it is utopian, it has less and less to do with the world, it looks inward'. And again, commenting on the situation in the late 1950s when Abstract Expressionism had become hugely successful and was being rapidly debased as a style by second-rate artists: 'It was hard to get a painting that was despicable enough so that no one would hang it – everybody was hanging everything. It was almost acceptable to hang a dripping paint rag, everybody was accustomed to this. The one thing everybody hated was commercial art; apparently they didn't hate that enough either.'

The problem was twofold: art had become inward-looking and unrealistic, and it had become debased through commercial exploitation. The Pop artists' solution was to bring art firmly back into contact with the world and with life, and to look for subject matter that would ensure a degree of unacceptability. It is one of the ironies of art history that, as Lichtenstein wryly points out in his final remark quoted above, Pop art in New York became at least as commercial as Abstract Expressionism, if not more so, and in less than half the time.

Roy Lichtenstein began his career as a painter about 1951 with pictures which were, in his own words, 'mostly reinterpretations of those artists concerned with the opening of the West, such as Remington, with a subject matter of cowboys, Indians, treaty signings'. From 1957 his work became Abstract Expressionist in the prevailing mode, but about 1960, he says, 'I began putting hidden comic images into those paintings, such as Mickey Mouse, Donald Duck and Bugs Bunny. At the same time I was drawing little Mickey Mouses and things for my children and working from bubble gum wrappers. I remember specifically. Then it occurred to me to do one of these bubble gum wrappers, as is, large just to see what it would look like.' The result, he found, was extremely interesting, and thus began his use of advertising and comic strip imagery which in the next few years was to make him one of the most prominent New York Pop artists. Asked why he chose to use such apparently degraded, unaesthetic source material, Lichtenstein spoke perhaps for all the Pop artists when he replied: 'I accept it as being there, in the world. . . . Signs and comic strips are interesting as subject matter. There are certain things that are useable, forceful and vital about commercial art.'

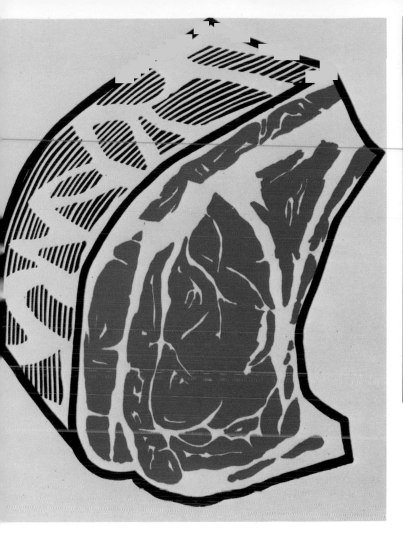

Roy Lichtenstein
Roto Broil 1961

Roy Lichtenstein
Chop 1962

Lichtenstein's early works drawn from advertising, *Roto Broil* (1961), *Chop* (1962), *Woman in Bath* (1963), reveal his striking ability to organize the crude but vital designs of his original sources into unified, powerful and coherent formal structures, while still retaining references to the original so strong that the spectator is constantly kept aware both of the figurative image, with its source (advertisements or comics), and of the traditional physical facts of painting – colour, line, form, composition and so on.

However, the formal, abstract message of Lichtenstein's painting was far from clear to everyone in the early days; many critics complained that he was simply blowing up comic strips and advertisements, that he did not 'transform' his sources. It is important to realize that Lichtenstein does alter his sources, although he still insists that he does not transform them. In 1963, replying to his critics, he said: 'Transformation is a strange word to use. It implies that art transforms. It doesn't, it just plain forms. Artists have never worked with the model – just with the painting. . . . My work is actually different from comic strips in that every mark is really in a different place, however slight the difference seems to some.'

Lichtenstein's working procedure is in fact, as follows: having located a source image he then makes a drawing or sketch of it (just as, for

Roy Lichtenstein
Woman in Bath 1963

example, John Constable would make a sketch of a particular piece of Suffolk landscape for later elaboration into a full-size painting). The purpose of the sketch is to recompose rather than reproduce the original, and although Lichtenstein says he tries to make as little change as possible he sometimes combines two or three sources into one image or even makes it up altogether. He then projects the drawing on to the canvas using an epidiascope and traces it in pencil. Further compositional adjustments may be made at this stage, before the dots are stencilled on, the colours applied and the characteristic thick black or blue lines put in. The dots in particular help to reproduce the feel of the printing process used for comic strips and advertisements, but Lichtenstein retains too the bright primaries and impersonal surfaces of his sources, and he once said that he wanted to hide the record of his hand.

The results of this procedure can be seen in *Roto Broil*, where the appliance itself, placed symmetrically against a uniform field of red, is treated in terms of bold simplified masses of black and white. Particularly striking is the rendering of the drainage holes in the frying-pan as black discs which take on a life of their own in the same way as they would in a completely abstract painting such as, for example, Vasarely's *Supernovae*. The symmetry of the composition is calculatedly broken by the black lines (paradoxically indicating highlights) on the right side of the appliance and by the protruding handle of the pan on the same side. And in *Woman in Bath* the prominent square grid contrasts strongly with the amazing system of flowing, swelling, organic linear forms which represents the girl's hair. This ability to create forms and compositions which are powerfully expressive in themselves yet remain readable as vivid representational images lies at the very core of Lichtenstein's genius and is the source of the extraordinary richness and complexity of his paintings.

Between 1963 and 1965 Lichtenstein produced two large groups of paintings which stand out from the rest of his work. In them forms, lines, colours, are increasingly abstract and expressive in themselves, and at the same time subject matter comes into greater prominence: based on romance and war comics respectively, these two groups of works deal with some of the fundamental dramas of human life. *M – Maybe* of 1965 depicts a girl (very attractive as in all Lichtenstein's love-comic paintings) waiting for a man (a theme taken up in a number of these works) in an imprecise but emphatically urban setting. Both her expression and the caption, 'M – Maybe he became ill and couldn't leave the studio', make it clear that she has been waiting a long time and is worried. Beyond that, like a Victorian narrative painter, Lichtenstein invites the spectator to speculate: who is the girl? who is the man with the studio? film star,

Roy Lichtenstein
Sweet Dreams, Baby

Roy Lichtenstein
As I Opened Fire . . . 1964

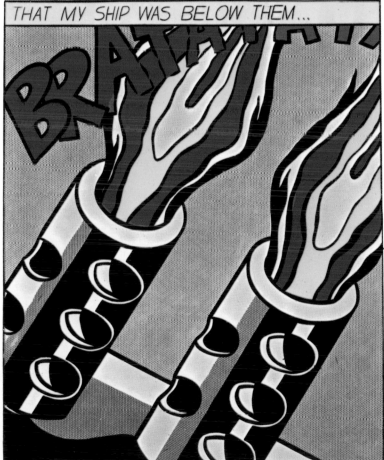

Roy Lichtenstein
Blonde Waiting 1964

photographer, broadcaster, artist even? and what is the nature of the
situation? has he stood her up for another woman? is he really ill? fatally
injured perhaps?

Sweet Dreams, Baby, like the war images, is an icon of aggression,
depicting as it does the single knockout blow that every man secretly
wishes he could deliver in answer to an insult, to settle an argument, to
win or protect a girl, and it refers to the American ideal of masculinity in
more ways than one: the fist is a very clear phallic symbol, and although
the recipient of the blow is a man the words of the caption, 'Sweet
dreams, baby!' could equally well be addressed to a girl and take on an
erotic implication. There is an interesting subgroup of the romance-comic
paintings which consists of paintings exclusively of girls' heads. One of
these is the *Blonde Waiting* of 1964, one of the most beautifully and most
strangely composed of all Lichtenstein's paintings, one of the masterpieces
of Pop.

Andy Warhol was born in Pittsburgh, USA, probably in 1928. He
went to Carnegie Institute of Technology in Pittsburgh from 1945 to
1949, then moved to New York where he remained. During the 1950s he
worked as a commercial artist and was highly successful, winning the Art
Directors' Club Medal for Shoe Advertisements in 1957. He had several
one-man exhibitions of drawings and published a number of books of
drawings on a variety of themes (cats and boys were two of them). His life

style at this time was affluent and elegant, and he collected art, having, it appears, a particular taste for Surrealist paintings (he owned works by Magritte among others).

In 1960, at the same time as, but quite independently of, Roy Lichtenstein, he began to make paintings based on comic strips and advertisements. One of the earliest of these is *Dick Tracy* of 1960, which still shows strong Abstract Expressionist influence: the caption is partially obscured by loosely brushed paint, drips of paint run down over Tracy's face, and that of his companion is treated partly as hard, comic-strip outline and partly again as loosely brushed paint. Thus, as in a work of Rauschenberg of the mid 1950s, popular imagery is still being integrated into a painterly structure, although Warhol is already presenting that imagery in a much more dispassionate manner than ever Rauschenberg

Andy Warhol
Dick Tracy 1960

Andy Warhol
Green Coca-Cola Bottles 1962

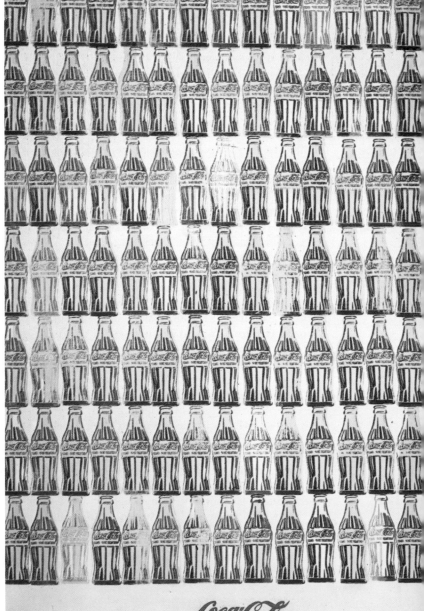

did. Unlike Lichtenstein, Warhol almost immediately abandoned comic-strip imagery, probably as being too anecdotal, and began to base his work on commercial and popular images that were much less obviously chosen by the artist with an eye to their content or visual quality. Indeed one of the crucial qualities of Warhol's images is their extreme obviousness: the most famous brands, Campbell's Soup, Coco-Cola; the most famous people, Elvis, Marilyn Monroe, Elizabeth Taylor; the most famous painting of the past, the Mona Lisa; the most familiar objects, dollar bills, newspapers. And when the individual image is chosen in itself an unfamiliar one, as with the car crashes, electric chairs, race riots, H-bomb explosions and so on, it always belongs to a category of images very familiar through the mass media. The effect of this choice of imagery is to give the baffling impression, even more strongly than in the case of Lichtenstein, that the artist has no interest in his images, that he is making no comment, that the images have no particular significance. Further, Warhol presented them in such a way that they appeared to have undergone little or no processing by the artist – they had not been 'transformed' into art, although his early paintings were in fact meticulously hand-done.

In 1962 he began to make his paintings by the silk-screen printing process, a sophisticated form of stencil usually used by artists for the multiple production of graphic work. Not only did he take the unprecedented step of using a printing process for the production of paintings but he adopted a recent commercial development of silk-screen printing whereby the image, instead of being laboriously cut by hand, is applied to the screen by photo-mechanical means. The actual printing Warhol did continue to do by hand, although it would often be carried out by an assistant under his supervision. In adopting this mechanical method Warhol seems to have simply been pursuing the logic of an art based on mass-produced imagery. But its effect, combined with the banality of his images, was to make his paintings appear completely meaningless, and this was reinforced by his frequent practice of repeating his images, often a large number of times, either on the same canvas or on separate canvases in series.

Of course, the paintings are not really meaningless. Warhol's images, in spite of their familiarity, in spite of their ready availability elsewhere than in his paintings, in spite, or even because, of their dispassionate presentation, remain extremely potent. His work, looked at overall, reveals certain constant and significant preoccupations with fame, with glamour, with death, with violence and disaster and with money. Nor do the images lack formal or aesthetic significance. Repetition is the means that Warhol used to reduce them to the status of elements in the composition – Cézanne's apples again. The spectator's attention is directed away from the image as such and towards a consideration of what the artist has done to it. A close scrutiny of say *200 Campbell's Soup* or *Marilyn Diptych*, both early silk-screen paintings, reveals that no single image is quite the same as any other. There are for example variations in paint texture and density which affect the detail, and the colours are sometimes out of register, producing distortions of form. Even *Cow Wallpaper* is more comic statement than mechanical repetition.

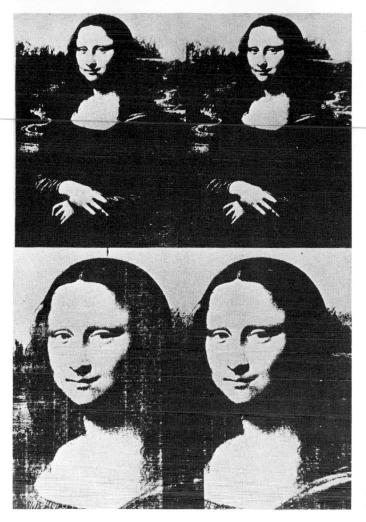

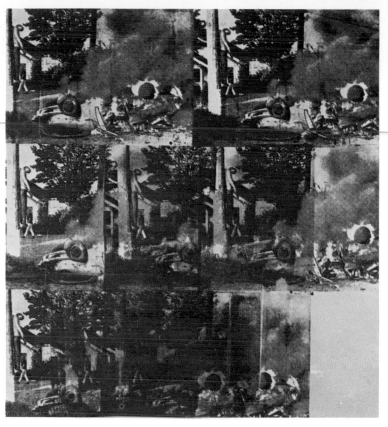

Andy Warhol
Green Disaster 1963

Andy Warhol
Four Mona Lisas 1963

As John Copland has pointed out, "Though the silk-screen process is simple many things can go wrong. For instance, if the medium is stroked across the image unevenly, if the density of the medium varies, if the squeegee is worn or dirty, or if there is insufficient medium to complete a stroke, the image will not print evenly. Parts of the image will become occluded or the dirt will print tracks, etc. The sharpness of the image will also vary according to the pressure exerted on the squeegee, or the angle it is held at. Many of these defficiencies will often work their way into the mesh and, unless the screen is cleaned, will show up in subsequent images. These normally accidental effects are often deliberately sought by Warhol.' So in Warhol's hands the silk-screen becomes a highly flexible means of creating expressive paint surfaces and forms. He exercised far more control over the production of his work than is generally supposed. As Richard Morphet tells us, 'Those who physically helped to make paintings in The Factory [Warhold's name for his studio] have explained how in even the most casual-seeming serial paintings Warhol was minutely concerned about the degree of painterly texture in background colours, and the exact choice of colour itself, not always taking it straight from the can but often mixing it into new hues and testing on strips of canvas until the desired shade was obtained'. Furthermore, Warhol

frequently heightened his screened images with touches of colour applied
with a brush (he did this in some of the *Marilyn* paintings for example);
and of course both the arrangement of the images (in regular rows, or
occasionally in slightly more complex configurations, as in *Mona Lisa
1963*, where some of the images are on their side) and the determining of
the relationship of the image or block of images to the ground are
conscious compositional procedures.

There is no doubt that the most striking formal aspect of Warhol's
painting is his vivid, varied and highly expressive use of colour, ranging
from the close correspondence to the original in *200 Campbell's Soup*
through the sinister monochrome washes of *Orange Disaster* and *Green
Disaster*, and the sumptuous and subtle harmony of orange, blue and
yellow of *Marilyn Diptych*, to the stunning variations (to which no

Andy Warhol
Pink Cow (Cow Wallpaper) 1966

Andy Warhol
Self-portrait 1967

reproduction can remotely do justice) of the *Marilyn* prints of 1967.
Finally, the almost complete dissolution of the image by intense and
vibrant colour takes place in the great *Self-Portraits* of 1967.

In these, among his last works before he abandoned painting for film
making and other activities, the wheel has turned full circle: after his first
portraits of Marilyn in 1962 Warhol himself became a star, a celebrity,
became in fact a subject for his own art. But these self-portraits must be
among the most self-effacing in the history of art: the image is difficult to
read, and deciphering it brings the realization that Warhol has based the
painting on a photograph taken with his hand in front of his face half
hiding it. Once again, and more forcibly than in any of his previous work,
he is directing our attention away from the image, to the painting as
something to look at in terms of coloured surfaces as you would look at a
Monet or a Matisse. As he himself said, 'I think painting is the same as it
has always been. It confuses me that people expect Pop art to make a
comment or say that its adherents merely accept their environment. I've
viewed most of the paintings I've ever loved – Mondrian's, Matisse's,
Pollock's – as being rather deadpan in that sense. All painting is fact and
that is enough; the paintings are charged with their very presence. The
situation, physical ideas, physical presence – I feel this is the comment';
and: 'If you want to know about Andy Warhol just look at the surface of

my paintings and films and me and there I am. There's nothing behind it.'

Claes Oldenburg was born in Sweden in 1929 and brought to the United States, where his father was on diplomatic service in New York, as a small child. In 1936 the family moved to Chicago, where Claes grew up and after taking a degree in Art and Literature at Yale University became an apprentice newspaper reporter. In 1952 he decided to become an artist and for two years attended the Art Institute of Chicago. In 1956 he moved to New York and settled on the Lower East Side, an area he has continued to live in, and which has exerted an important influence on him. From the beginning he had an exceptionally strong sense of engagement with the urban environment, 'the experience of the city', but in a significantly different aspect of it from those which had drawn the attention of Lichtenstein and Warhol: 'The streets, in particular, fascinated me. They seemed to have an existence of their own where I discovered a whole world of objects that I had never known before. Ordinary packages became sculptures in my eye, and I saw street refuse as elaborate accidental compositions.'

The results of this activity, his first mature works, were shown in two exhibitions at the Judson Gallery in 1959 and 1960. The second of these exhibitions was actually called 'The Street', and consisted of figures, signs and objects constructed from discarded or fragile materials: cardboard, paper, sacking, string. Many of the works were *Ray Guns* – strange objects made in a variety of materials but based on the ray gun of space comics, a kind of mascot and basic form for Oldenburg that engenders endless variations. It is a symbol of the city itself – Ray Gun spelt backwards is Nug Yar, which Oldenburg says sounds to him like New York – and as a phallic symbol also it relates to another of Oldenburg's fundamental preoccupations: the erotic. Taken as a whole, the exhibition was an extraordinary poetic evocation of the city through the medium of some of its humblest and least valued materials.

In the autumn of 1960, recalls Oldenburg, 'I drove around the city one day with Jimmy Dine. By chance we drove through Orchard Street, both sides of which are packed with small stores. As we drove I remember having a vision of 'The Store'. I saw, in my mind's eye a complete environment based on this theme. Again it seemed to me that I had discovered a new world, I began wandering through stores – all kinds and all over – as though they were museums. I saw the objects displayed in windows and on counters as precious works of art.'

In late summer 1961, Oldenburg moved to a studio in East Second Street which became 'The Store', filled with sculptures of food, clothing and other objects, made mainly of chicken-wire and plaster-soaked muslin or sacking, cheap and commonplace materials as before. In September 1962 he extended the idea of 'The Store' in a second version shown at the Green Gallery.

'The Store' sculptures were brightly, even vividly painted. Their colour is a very significant aspect of them; they are paintings as well as sculptures – and, as Oldenburg has stated, the paints themselves carry a direct reference to their source in the urban store: 'The Street was a metaphor for line. The Store became a metaphor for colour. In an East

Side paint store, I found a line of paints, Frisco Enamel, which came in seven particularly bright colours that seemed to symbolize the store to me. These colours became my palette. The paint would be used straight from the can without any mixing or blending of colour to paint reliefs of store objects.'

These works – *Giant Blue Pants, Breakfast Table, Kitchen Stove, White Shirt and Blue Tie* are a few of them – do not, as a work by Warhol or Lichtenstein does, refer you immediately to their source in the outside world. Some of them, it is true, incorporate real objects – the stove and the table for example – but these are primarily a means of display, like a sculpture pedestal in a museum. The effect of the reliefs of the store objects themselves is to stimulate the imagination. They are pants, shirt, food; but they could also be almost anything else, or simply abstract shapes, accumulations of plaster and paint. This effect has been well

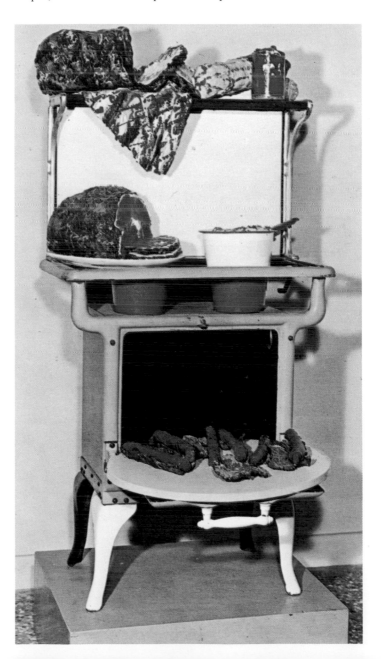

Claes Oldenburg
Kitchen Stove 1962

described (as reported by the critic Rublowsky) by a visitor to
Oldenburg's studio who noticed an object he had made. 'It was a vaguely
wedge-shaped piece of plaster crudely spattered with aluminium paint.
He picked it up and tried to identify it. "It's a lady's handbag," he said,
as he turned the object about his hand. "No, it's an iron. No, it's a
typewriter. No, it's a toaster. No, a piece of pie." Oldenburg was
delighted: the object, which was nothing more than a shape the artist had
been toying with, was exactly what the visitor had described. All the
objects he named were embodied in that small wedge-shaped bit of
plaster.'

This equivalence of form, the way in which one form can
simultaneously relate to many other forms, fascinates Oldenburg and is
the basis of his art.

In the second 'Store' exhibition Oldenburg showed a number of
sculptures which differed from those in the rest of the show, and from his
earlier works, in two important ways. Some of them had been enormously
scaled up, like the *Hamburger, Popsicle, Price*, which is three feet (0.9m)

Claes Oldenburg
Hamburger, Popsicle, Price 1962

Claes Oldenburg
Giant Soft Swedish Light Switch 1966

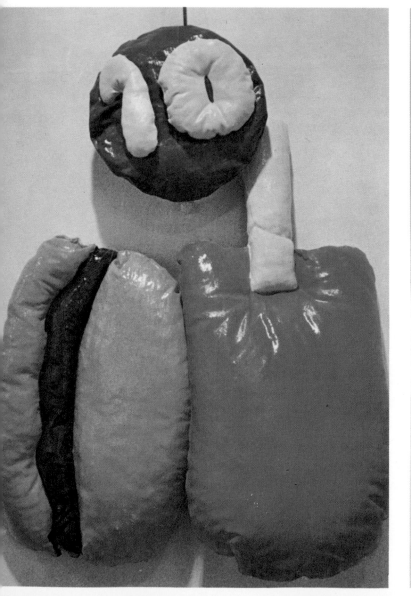

Claes Oldenburg
Giant Fireplug 1969

Claes Oldenburg
Trowel Scale B 1971

high; and some of these were, a thing unprecedented in the history of sculpture, soft and yielding rather than hard and unchanging. One of the earliest of these soft sculptures was the *Floorburger (Giant Hamburger)* of 1962, which is seven feet (2.13m) across and a little over four feet (1.21m) thick. It is made of canvas filled with foam and cardboard and painted.

Both these changes related to Oldenburg's interest in the equivalence of forms. The change in scale of the hamburger opens up a whole new range of references, and, by removing the art object even further from its original source, draws the spectator's attention even more strongly than before to the purely sculptural qualities of the work: its shape, colour, texture and so on. This concern for scale culminated in the plans for giant monuments which Oldenburg drew up from 1965 onwards. These monuments are colossal versions either of street furniture, like the *Giant Fireplug* which Oldenburg has imagined placed in the Civic Centre in

Chicago, or of everyday objects, like the *Trowel Scale B*, one of the regrettably few Oldenburg monuments to have been built and installed.

The change from hard to soft was even more far-reaching; for a soft sculpture does not just passively refer to other forms but can actually metamorphose, change its shape. A soft sculpture by Oldenburg never looks the same in successive installations; and while it remains installed the action of gravity produces gradual changes: Oldenburg actually harnesses a fundamental natural force as part of the sculptural process. The *Giant Soft Swedish Light Switch* of 1966, with its mysterious sagging forms, is a marvellous example of this.

Claes Oldenburg has tried to create an art which is universal in its significance. Taking his point of departure from the specific and familiar in everyday life, he has attempted to make sculptures which stand for everything: sculptures that are embodiments of and metaphors for the whole of life. That this is his aim is made quite clear in his statement, one of the most moving manifestos in the history of modern art, first published in 1961:

'I am for an art that is political–erotical–mystical, that does something other than sit on its ass in a museum.

'I am for an art that grows up not knowing it is art at all, an art given the chance of having a starting point of zero.

'I am for an art that embroils itself with the everyday crap & still comes out on top.

'I am for an art that imitates the human, that is comic, if necessary, or violent or whatever is necessary.

'I am for an art that takes its forms from the lines of life itself, that twists and extends and accumulates and spits and drips and is heavy and coarse and blunt and sweet and stupid as life itself.'

James Rosenquist studied art at the University of Minnesota from 1952 to 1955. During one of his summer vacations he took a job with an industrial decorating company, travelling through the Midwest painting the outsides of warehouses and enormous grain storage bins. In 1955 he won a scholarship to the Art Students' League in New York where he completed his studies. In the following years he supported himself in a number of different jobs, but in particular he worked for some time painting billboards for an advertising company. Both the industrial decorating and the billboard painting clearly had a considerable effect on his development as an artist, affecting his subject matter, the overall scale of his work, and particularly his sense of scale *within* the painting, as well as his highly individual way of composing.

Recalling the first of his jobs, Rosenquist said: 'Now picture this scene: there's this stretch of wall at least as big as a football field and way down in one corner is this man with a bucket of paint.' Speaking of the time he worked on the thirty- by one-hundred-foot billboard of the Astor-Victoria cinema in Times Square, he said that he had the opportunity 'to see things in a new relationship'. Working on a particular bit of figure or letter of the alphabet, 'you couldn't see the whole thing at once, it was like infinity . . . everything looked different'. These statements have a direct reference to the pictorial devices used in Rosenquist's paintings like *I Love You with my Ford* (1961), one of his earlier masterpieces, in which

James Rosenquist
I Love You with my Ford 1961

enormous out-of-focus fragments of Ford motor car, girl's face, spaghetti
in tomato, are brought together to express the erotic theme implied in the
title: the Ford phallic symbol looms over the face of the girl, her eyes
closed and lips parted in ecstasy, while below the consummation is
somehow symbolized by the writhing, glutinous masses of spaghetti.
Rosenquist's pictures reflect his own experience of billboard painting, but
they also reflect the similarly fragmented kaleidoscopic visual experience
of the city dweller as he walks through busy streets with buildings and
hoardings towering over him or catches a brief glimpse of them from the
windows of a car or bus.

Tom Wesselmann's university career was sporting rather than scholarly
or artistic, and it was only when he was drafted into the army that he
began to learn to draw, with the ambition of becoming a cartoonist. With
this in mind, after leaving the army he enrolled at the Cincinnati Art
Academy and then spent from 1957 to 1960 at the Cooper Union art
school in New York. It was there that he discovered painting and the
world of art, and towards the end of his final year he abandoned
cartooning altogether and turned his whole attention to painting and
collage. His early collages involved old newspapers, rags, leaves and old
package labels used for the sake of their colour and texture, but a crucial

Tom Wesselmann
Great American Nude no. 99 1968

development in his art took place in 1960 when he began to use collage
elements to represent themselves, and combined them with paint in works
dealing in a new way with two traditional themes – the nude and the
still-life. The subjects of his still-lifes are taken from billboard
advertisements for food, drink, cigarettes and consumer durables (these
last often represented by the real thing, so well integrated into the
composition that it is difficult to tell whether it is painted or not).

Wesselmann's nudes, most of which belong to the series of *Great
American Nudes* which he started in 1962 and is still continuing, derive
their formal strength and qualities from Matisse, an important influence
on Wesselmann; but they refer also to the soft-core porn glamour nude of
the *Playboy* type of magazine. However, they are often both more frankly
and more effectively erotic than any *Playboy* nude; and perhaps
Wesselmann's greatest achievement has been to fill a long-standing gap in
the history of art by fully eroticizing the nude in 'high-art' painting.

Robert Indiana uses words as images, and presents them in his
paintings, not only as forceful visual experiences but also as injunctions,
slogans or messages to the spectator. These words relate to the American
Dream and other aspects of American life which, however, Indiana does
not accept without comment. It is pretty hard to swallow the whole thing
about the American Dream. It started the day the Pilgrims landed, the
dream, the idea that Americans have more to eat than anyone else. But I
remember going to bed without enough to eat.' In his 1961 painting
titled *The American Dream*, and in the later *Demuth Five*, the dream is seen
in terms of a pinball game where winner takes all and a false move brings
up the tilt sign. Using hard-edged imagery taken from the pinball
machine, and flat areas of very bright colour, Indiana incorporates his
message in a particularly abstract, impersonal and deadpan form, and he
once said: 'I still use a brush because I have not found a machine

inexpensive enough to take its place.' Other paintings simply proclaim
EAT, DIE, HUG, ERR, or, most famous of all, with its flat interlocking areas
of shimmering complementary colours, LOVE.

Allan D'Arcangelo had his first exhibition in New York in 1963, by
which time Pop art was thoroughly established. However, he at once
made his own a particular area of imagery – the American highway –

Robert Indiana
The Demuth Five 1963

Robert Indiana
Love 1967

Allan D'Arcangelo
Highway no. 2 1963

and has produced a whole series of paintings like *Highway No. 2* (1963), in which the immense distances of the United States are romantically evoked through the use of zooming perspective and the imagery of road signs. Like Robert Indiana, D'Arcangelo paints in an extremely tight, flat manner, his imagery always subsumed in a precise geometric composition.

The West Coast

American Pop art was created and developed in New York, but found rapid and early acceptance and a particular individual character on the West Coast, where activity was focused on the two centres of Los Angeles in the south and San Francisco in the north. Los Angeles emerged as the more important centre, and was the first to recognize the genius of Andy Warhol, giving him his first one-man show as a fully fledged Pop artist in 1962. The city of Los Angeles itself, perhaps the most extraordinary urban environment in the world, was an important influence on West Coast Pop, and it is also, of course, the home of Hollywood, itself an important influence on Pop art everywhere. Equally significant were the various exotic subcultures that flourish in the area: those of the surfer, the hot-rodders, the drag-racers, the car customizers and the outlow motor cycle clubs like Satan's Slaves and, most famous of all, Hell's Angels.

Commemorated in the title of Tom Wolfe's essay *The Kandy Kolored Tangerine Flake Streamline Baby*, the amazing paint jobs and baroque bodywork created by the car customizers and the elaborate decorations of the California surfboards are examples of an industrial folk art of great impact and brilliance which set the tone for much West Coast Pop art. So too were the bizarre drag-racing cars and hot rods, and so was the Hell's Angels' 'chopped hog', a Harley-Davidson 74 which in the hands of the Angels was stripped down and rebuilt to become virtually a mobile piece of sculpture. The Angels' uniform was also a rich item of folk art, particularly the sleeveless denim jacket bearing the 'colours': a winged skull wearing a motor cycle helmet with the name Hell's Angels above with, below, the letters MC and the local chapter name, e.g. San Bernardino. These jackets were further decorated with chains, swastikas and other signs, slogans and emblems: such as the number 13 (indicating use of marijuana), and the notorious red wings.

The world of customizing and of the big bikes is strongly reflected in the work of one of the two major Los Angeles Pop artists. Billy Al Bengston has worked since 1960 on a series of paintings of chevrons and motor-bike badges and parts treated as heraldic devices, the images placed centrally on the canvas and painted in glowing colours with immaculate precision and a high degree of finish. About 1962 his painting took on an even greater richness and gloss, when he began to use sprayed cellulose paint on hardboard and later actually on sheets of metal, thus getting even closer to the technique and medium of his sources. Some of these metal sheet works are artfully crumpled, thus adding a suggestion of accident and death to the glamorous perfection of the painted emblem.

The other major Los Angeles Pop artist is Ed Ruscha (pronounced, the artist insists, as Ruschay). He began using Pop imagery (packaging) in

Edward Ruscha
Standard Station, Amarillo, Texas 1963

1960 in paintings like *Box Smashed Flat*, where presentation of commercial imagery and what looks like Edwardian commercial lettering is still combined with a painterly style. But his painting quickly took on an almost inhuman exquisiteness, precision and perfection of finish, as in *Noise . . .* of 1963.

   Like Indiana, Ruscha is fascinated by words, and these have always formed the principal subject matter of his paintings and graphics. In some works the words appear in isolation floating against backgrounds of beautifully graded colour that give a feeling of infinite coloured space. Sometimes associated images are introduced, such as the cocktail olive in *Sin*, and somtimes the word is given a specific context, as with the company names (e.g. 'Standard') for which the architecture becomes a

Edward Ruscha
Noise, Pencil, Broken Pencil, Cheap Western
1963

setting in Ruscha's garage paintings (*Standard Station, Amarillo, Texas*). One lithograph, where the word Hollywood streams unforgettably out of the sunset in the steep zooming perspective and giant lettering of wide-screen title sequences, exemplifies the manner in which Ruscha depicts his words in such a way that their meaning is conveyed pictorially as well as verbally.

Garages·in themselves are one of Ruscha's most important motifs after words. They first appear in his work in 1962, not in painting or graphic work, but in a book: *Twenty-six Gasoline Stations*, consisting of 26 absolutely deadpan, factual, non-arty photographs of Western garages. The attitude behind these photographs comes very close to that of the New York Pop artists, and especially Warhol: the acceptance of aspects of the world which no one had considered in an art context before. *Twenty-six Gasoline Stations* was followed by *Various Small Fires* (1964), *Some Los Angeles Apartments* (1965), *On the Sunset Strip* (1966, a twenty-seven foot fold-out continuous photograph of every building on the Strip), *Thirty-four Parking Lots* (1967) and others. As with Warhol's work, the nature of the motif eventually directs the spectator's attention to the manner of its presentation. Ruscha's books are beautiful visual objects, models of cool elegance and immaculate typography, finely printed in limited editions at the artist's expense, although there is little of the connoisseur in his attitude towards them; asked once about the expense of production he replied: 'It's almost worth the money to have the thrill of seeing 400 exactly identical books stocked in front of you.' In the end it seems certain that these will be his most significant contribution to Pop art.

In North California, Pop art was similarly dominated by two major artists, who, like Bengston and Ruscha, have a certain amount in common both in their technique and in the way they handle their imagery.

Wayne Thiebaud employs thick, luscious and brilliantly hued paint to depict, as he says, 'Things which I feel have been overlooked. Maybe a lollypop tree has not seemed like a thing worth painting because of its banal references.' Thiebaud's subject matter consists mainly but not exclusively of cakes, sweets, pies, ice-creams and similar goodies which he presents in the usual deadpan, frontal or repetitive way of Pop art. But the way he actually paints these items is unique to Thiebaud: he uses the paint not to depict them illusionistically but to recreate their textures and colours. Thiebaud has explained that his interest is in 'what happens when the relationship between paint and subject matter comes as close as I can get it – white, gooey, shiny, sticky oil paint spread out on top of a painted cake to 'become' frosting [icing]. It is playing with reality – making an illusion which grows out of an exploration of the propensities of materials.' *Refrigerator Pies* (1962) is typical of Thiebaud's work; and if in the end his paintings, like this one, have a highly synthetic as well as edible look about them it is because his source material itself is largely synthetic.

Mel Ramos uses similarly luscious paint but to rather different ends: he does not imitate textures like Thiebaud, nor does he interest himself in the same type of subject matter. After an early phase about 1962–63 of painting comic-book heroes and heroines, Ramos quickly found his own

Wayne Thiebaud
Refrigerator Pies 1962

specific and personal iconography of nude pin-up girls. These young
ladies are depicted by Ramos in often quite explicit sexual situations with
either appropriately phallic forms of packaging, consumer goods or food
like Coca-Cola bottles, cigarettes (in *Philip Morris*), a corn cob (in *Miss
Corn Flakes*) or, particularly in later works, with various animals, either
symbolically phallic such as weasels and pelicans, traditionally highly-
sexed like monkeys, or simply representative of brute maleness – gorillas
for example. *Ode to Ang* plays a favourite Pop game with high art (the
source is Ingres); and in depictions of girls with pumas and other big cats
he has extended his range of erotic feeling by introducing an element of
refined, almost decadent perversion. Ramos's art is probably intended as

Mel Ramos
Philip Morris 1965

Mel Ramos
Ode to Ang 1972

mild parody of the obvious Freudianism of Madison Avenue, but there is
no doubt that it is also extremely enjoyable for what it is: light hearted,
witty, glamorous, very high-quality pornography.

Great Britain

By the time artists in the USA began to take up modern urban culture
and its imagery as a source for their art, Pop art had already established
itself in Great Britain and embarked on an entirely distinct and separate
development which was influenced by American life, as seen through the
mass media, but not by American art. In the late 1940s two artists
emerged who were to have an important influence on the development of
British Pop art. These two precursors were Francis Bacon and Eduardo
Paolozzi.

From 1949 onwards Bacon began to use photographs, from mass-media sources among others, as a basis for his paintings. They were always considerably transformed, it is true, but Lawrence Alloway, a critic who was around when these paintings first appeared, has written of the earliest of them, the series of screaming heads of 1949, that 'the photographic reference was conspicuous and much discussed at the time'. The source image for these (and many later works) was a still from Eisenstein's film *Battleship Potemkin* (1925), a close up of the face of the wounded nurse in the Odessa steps massacre sequence. He later moved on to using photographs by Eadweard Muybridge, made in the 1880s, of animals and humans in motion, and another major source has been *Positioning in Radiography*, a medical textbook on the making of X-ray photographs.

At the same time as he began to use photographs, Bacon also established the practice of basing paintings on works of art from the past. Here, one of his most important sources has been a reproduction of the famous portrait of Pope Innocent X by Velázquez in the Palazzo Doria in Rome, although significantly enough Bacon has never seen the original, and once, when he was in Rome, did not take the opportunity to do so.

Above all, Bacon combines in his paintings powerfully evocative images with equally forceful formal statements. Painting, he wrote in 1953, should be concerned 'with attempting to make idea and technique inseparable. Painting in this sense tends towards a complete interlocking of image and paint, so that the image is the paint and vice versa. Here the brush stroke creates the form and does not merely fill it in. Consequently every movement of the brush on the canvas alters the shape and implication of the image.' In spite of the clarity of his published views, many of his early critics discussed Bacon's work exclusively in terms of its imagery, ignoring its formal statement, just as they later did with the work of the Pop artists.

Finally, as Alloway has pointed out, 'Bacon was the only painter of an earlier generation who was regarded with respect by the younger artists in London. Moore, Nicholson, Pasmore, Sutherland . . . were considered to be irrelevant to any new art in the 1950s'. An important reason for this respect was the tough, uncompromising quality of his art and indeed its positive offensiveness to the then current standards of taste. Even as late as 1962 it was possible for one of London's leading critics to write of Bacon: 'Cruelty, ambiguous sex, a penchant for the perverse, all these occur in his art . . . he both gloats over the unusual and derives stimulus from the decadence he paints.' Any older artist capable of evoking this kind of response must have appealed greatly to the rebellious young.

While Francis Bacon stands as a father figure to British Pop art, Eduardo Paolozzi, born in Edinburgh of Italian immigrant parents in 1924, played a direct and crucial part in its development. From the earliest steps of his art education at Edinburgh College of Art, where he went in 1941, Paolozzi displayed a strong interest in popular culture and drew disapproval from his teachers for copying pictures of aeroplanes, footballers and film stars. At this time he also began making collages of material taken from magazines and other sources, including images from science fiction, aviation technology, advertisements for food, domestic

1960s, were looking at Pop sources but using them as the basis for a completely abstract art. Smith left the Royal College in 1957, went to America, where he stayed until 1961, and there developed a painterly, large-scale art rooted in the mass-media but in which the source material was not presented (as it always is in true Pop art) as a strongly figurative image. Rather, certain of its qualities, of colour or of shape, were isolated as the basis for the painting. In his series of cigarette-packet paintings of the early 1960s, for example, form and colour are derived from the packet itself, and the large scale and soft-focus treatment come from wide-screen cinema cigarette advertisements where a packet may appear six feet high and, when viewed from close to, dissolves into blurred and shifting washes of colour.

Smith has explained that he wanted to extend the expressive range of painting, to create a new kind of fine art experience through the use of commercial art: 'This would be possible, I thought, through paintings that shared scale, colour, texture, almost a shared *matière* with an aspect of the mass-media.' This attitude in itself must have been influential, but Smith's paintings also demonstrated to the younger Pop artists not only a new sense of scale, quite different from that of Hamilton and Blake, but also the possibility of a broad painterly treatment of Pop source material.

David Hockney, like Allen Jones, has recorded his appreciation of R. B. Kitaj, who, he says, has affected him more than anyone else 'not only as an artist but as a person'. Other influences on Hockney were Francis Bacon and the French artist Jean Dubuffet, who may well have drawn his attention to the aesthetic possibilities of the most important of his early stylistic sources, graffiti, an aspect of the urban scene not really looked at by any other Pop artist. Indeed, although the debt to Bacon, especially, is apparent in Hockney's work in the early 1960s, its primary visual quality comes from the extraordinary graffiti-like drawing of the figures and from the scrawled messages and individual words, parts of words and numbers which in some cases come to dominate the painting. (Hockney has explained that he wrote on many of his paintings at this time in order to make his meaning as clear as possible.) His paintings also have the usual Pop characteristic of combining strongly abstract elements with vivid figurative imagery. In, for example, *The Cha Cha Cha that was Danced in the Early Hours of the 24th March* (1961), one of his best early paintings, the dancing figure and the words and messages are set against flat rectangles of emblematic red and blue at the top of the picture, a large expanse of raw untouched canvas in the middle and a flat strip of mauve at the lower edge.

The subject matter of Hockney's art is broadly autobiographical, and in the early 1960s, while still at the Royal College, his principal preoccupations, not surprisingly perhaps, were with art, and the making of art, and sex. These themes come strongly through in his painting, even when, as in another major early work, his shaped canvas painting of a Ty-Phoo tea packet, he is ostensibly concerned with that other major Pop subject, packaging and advertising imagery. In particular, the title of this work, *Tea Painting in an Illusionistic Style*, draws attention to the formal statement, while the artist's erotic interests are expressed in the life-size figure of a naked boy who appears (part of the whole illusionistic joke of

David Hockney
Tea Painting in an Illusionistic Style 1962

David Hockney
California Seascape 1968

the painting) to be actually sitting inside the packet. Further evidence of
the way in which Hockney at this time was taking the language of
painting as part of his subject matter is provided by the fact that he
exhibited the Ty-Phoo picture in 1962 under the title *Demonstration of
Versatility – Tea Painting in an Illusionistic Style*. It is one of four
Demonstrations, another of which, *A Grand Procession of Dignitaries in the
Semi-Egyptian Style*, also marks his first (but by no means his last) use of
earlier art as a source.

There is no doubt that David Hockney was the dominant personality
in the Royal College group, and he has had a greater success than any of
them. In fact his brilliant success and his personal style have made him,

like Andy Warhol in America, a Pop star himself; and many of his later
paintings depict the surroundings of successful Pop personalities –
California Seascape, and the series of California swimming pools, for
example – as well as the personalities themselves.

Allen Jones, like David Hockney, gained a rapid success after the 1961
'Young Contemporaries' exhibition. His earliest themes were, in rather
odd contrast, sex on the one hand and buses, aeroplanes and parachutists
on the other. His style was both painterly and abstract, closer to Richard
Smith in its approach than any of the other artists of the Royal College
group (although, as we have seen, Kitaj was also important to him). As
well as adopting a painterly approach, Jones also used the important
formal device of the shaped canvas. In his famous series of bus paintings
of 1962–63, many of the canvases are staggered rectangles that seem to
lean forward along the wall, physically implying movement; and in a
number of them, too, the wheels were painted on a separate piece of
canvas and literally attached to the bottom of the canvas. The effect of
this is to give the image a greater reality and impact than it could have if
simply depicted as a figure on a ground.

Erotic imagery first appeared in two *Bikini* paintings in 1962, although
these were still, like the bus paintings, very abstract. The eroticism
became explicit in paintings of couples and hermaphrodites like *Man–
Woman* (1963), and in the single figure pin-up girls like *Curious Woman*
(1964), which has the breasts actually modelled in three dimensions.
Later Jones's obsession became more intense, and he expressed it in a
much tighter, glossier style than before. His sources lie particularly in
those sex magazines catering for underwear, rubber and leather fetishists,
and in 1969 he produced a number of pieces of erotic furniture consisting
of very realistically modelled and glamorous girls wearing leather boots

Derek Boshier
Identi-Kit Man 1962

Allen Jones
Girl Table 1969

Antony Donaldson
Girl Sculpture (Gold and Orange) 1970

and harness, offering themselves as seats, hatstands and *Girl Tables*.

Derek Boshier was the third member of the Royal College group to adopt a painterly semi-abstract approach to painting Pop imagery, but right from the beginning he tended to blend passages of extreme painterliness with bold, clear cut figurative images. In *Identi-Kit Man* (1962), one of his very best early works, the raw canvas is beautifully brushed with long feathery strokes of white, blue and mauve to create an effect of pale atmospheric colour which contrasts strongly with the flat, sharply outlined giant green toothbrushes and the vivid red and white stripes of the toothpaste. It is clear that the heraldic quality of the striped toothpaste made a strong appeal to Boshier, and in the next few years he evolved a kind of bright jazzy painting based on such sources but from which all figurative references were eliminated. Since 1964 he has been a completely abstract artist.

Anthony Donaldson was at the Slade School, and did not develop a fully-fledged pop iconography and treatment until about a year later than the Royal College group. But from 1962 he produced brightly coloured paintings, based mostly on repeated images of strippers, in which the tones are manipulated in such a way as to produce a constant strong image-ground reversal which makes the painting extremely abstract in its effect. By 1963 he was producing jazzy, optically active works in which the imagery was no longer readable, although there were still strong references to the source. Later his work became more figurative and more specifically erotic, and *Girl Sculpture* (1970) effectively combines the sensuality of the nude girl with the extreme sensuousness of a beautiful gold flake acrylic paint job.

Superficially Patrick Caulfield is the British artist who appears to be the closest to Roy Lichtenstein: he presents, like Lichtenstein, boldly outlined figurative images which in fact are part of a rigorously abstract formal structure. However, his imagery has none of the assertiveness usual in Pop art, and he does not draw on advertising or indeed any of the

Patrick Caulfield
Pottery 1969

Right:

Eduardo Paolozzi
The Last of the Idols 1963

Far right:

Joe Tilson
Transparency Clip-O-Matic Lips 1968

usual Pop sources. Instead he uses images which, while being instantly familiar and recognizable, as in *Pottery*, for example, are so extremely unassertive as to emphasize to a degree greater than in any Pop artist the purely formal message of the work.

Having played a major part in laying the foundation of Pop art in Britain in the 1950s, Paolozzi insists that he is not a Pop artist and that, if anything, he is a Surrealist. However, it is almost impossible to look at Pop art in Britain in the 1950s and not to take his work into account,

particularly his striking sculptures based on machinery and the heavy industrial aspects of the city landscape like electricity sub-stations. *The Last of the Idols* (1963) combines solid architectural forms with a wheel, is topped off with what looks like a heavy electrical insulator and has a hard paint finish like that of heavy machinery.

Significantly these works (from 1962 onwards) were made for Paolozzi at an engineering works near Ipswich, and they are assembled (welded) either from stock machine parts available from manufacturer's catalogues or from machine parts made to Paolozzi's own specifications. More than any Pop artist, Paolozzi has pursued the logic of using industrial processes to make an art whose source itself lies in the industrial world.

Like Paolozzi, Joe Tilson is an artist whose sources lay in the urban, industrial and commercial scene, but whose aesthetic aims in almost all his work of the 1960s were very different from those of the Pop artists. However, Tilson made a number of purely Pop works, in particular the series of *Transparencies* started in 1967 and including images of Yuri Gagarin, Che Guevara and the Five Senses, one of which, *Transparency Clip-O-Matic Lips*, with its huge glistening mouth and gleaming teeth, is a stunning presentation (relating more to the erotic than to the sense of taste which it is supposed to represent) of an image presumably culled from a toothpaste ad.

Continental Europe

It has frequently been pointed out that true Pop art, both for sociological and intellectual reasons, is an Anglo-Saxon phenomenon. But the revolt against Abstract Expressionism which gave rise to Pop art in America found its counterpart in Continental Europe at the same time, and produced a kind of art clearly related to Pop. This art is best understood in the context of *Nouveau Réalisme* or New Realism, a movement founded originally in 1960 by the French critic Pierre Restany and a small group of artists (among them, Yves Klein and Arman); the term quickly came to be applied to any artist following this tendency, whether he was a member of Restany's original group or not.

Restany published the first manifesto of New Realism in April 1960 in Milan (New Realism was to operate mainly on a French–Italian axis, with the Germans keeping somewhat to themselves). In it he stated in florid rhetoric his rejection of the existing situation in art: 'We are witnessing today the exhaustion and sclerosis of every existing vocabulary, of all the languages, of all the styles', and then went on to propose a remedy. 'What are we going to put in their place? The fascinating adventure of the real seen as itself and not through the prism of an imaginative and intellectual transcription.' In spite of the firmness with which Restany asserts that there will be no imaginative or intellectual transformation of the source material, there is no doubt that the basic attitude of the New Realists towards urban reality was both intellectual and romantic, whereas that of the Anglo-Saxon Pop artists was intellectual and *cool*, i.e. classic. This is made clear by Restany himself in the second manifesto, published in Paris in 1961: 'The New Realists consider the world as a picture, the great fundamental masterpiece from which they take fragments endowed with universal significance.' This significance, for Restany, was a sociological one: 'And through these specific images the whole social reality, the common wealth of human activity, the great republic of our social intercourse, of our social activity, is brought before us.'

This second manifesto of New Realism bore the title 'Forty Degrees above Dada', a clear acknowledgment of Restany's debt to that movement, and especially to Duchamp. Like the American and British Pop artists, he took his point of departure from the readymade. 'In the present context,' he wrote, 'Duchamp's readymades take on a new significance. They translate the right to direct expression of a whole organic sector of modern life, that of the city, the street, the factory, of mass production. . . . The anti-art gesture of Duchamp will henceforth be *affirmative*. . . . The readymade is no longer the height of negativity but the basis of a new expressive vocabulary.'

There is no doubt that the most original and the most influential of the New Realists was Yves Klein, who died prematurely in 1962. His aims were, ultimately, quite different from those of the rest of the group. Klein's works which have most relevance to New Realism are his *Anthropometries*, paintings of the female nude made by applying the paint direct to the girl's body and imprinting her on the canvas. Klein's real concern was not with the external world but with the reality of art, and

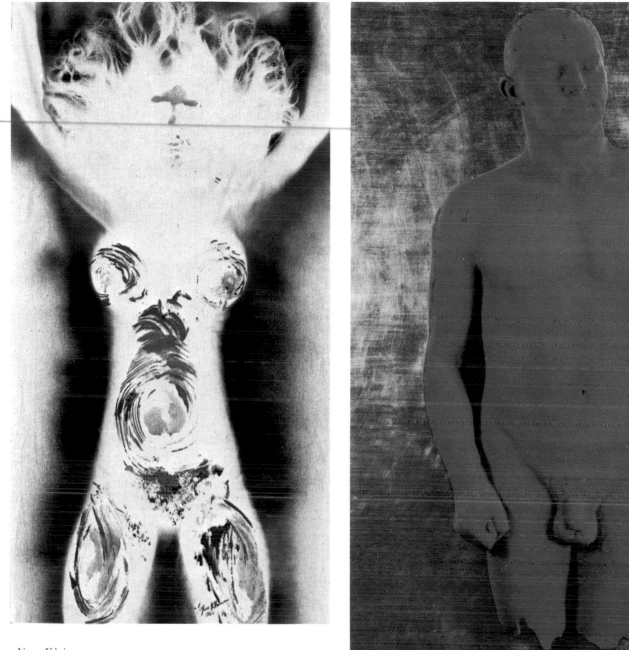

Yves Klein
Suaire ANT-SU 2 (Anthropometry) 1962

Yves Klein
Relief (Arman) 1962

particularly with the reality of colour, which he felt embodied the essence of art. From 1949 onwards he produced a large number of monochrome paintings in pink, blue and gold, and finally, in 1957, settled on blue as representing the essence of colour. In the last few years of his life he produced a series of 194 paintings in an unearthly, pure ultramarine blue which became known to the art world simply as IKB – International Klein Blue. Being the essence of art, this blue could be applied to any support, and *Lecturer IKB Elegant* is one of the many works Klein made basically from sponges soaked in his blue. His portrait of Arman, a cast of

8 Pluralism since 1960

MARCO LIVINGSTONE

Increasingly through the twentieth century, and especially after the stranglehold exerted by Abstract Expressionism, powerful and idiosyncratic art has often been made against the prevailing ethos and in response not to theory but to a desire for directness and immediacy of experience. Nevertheless the proliferation of new movements at an ever accelerating pace has been one of the most marked characteristics of art since the early 1960s. The tendency for artists to react consciously against the tenets of their immediate predecessors, combined with their need to combat the isolation of the studio through friendship with other colleagues, has led repeatedly to the formation of new groupings often further encouraged by critics, dealers and museum administrators keen to be first at the scene of every new artistic development. There has been a widespread anxiety not to be left behind, like the conservatives who had resisted the rise of Modernism at the turn of the century. This has engendered an atmosphere conducive to experiments remote from the taste of the public at large. The pressures of a constantly growing and more powerful market for contemporary art during this period have likewise exercised a strong influence, especially in the United States, which has come to dominate a more genuinely international art world both in terms of its art criticism and the commercial gallery system centered in New York City. The effects of economic forces have been manifest not only in a sometimes grotesque parody of the built-in obsolescence of the consumer society, which requires new status-bearing products every season, but in the reaction of artists who have sought to subvert the system altogether by abandoning the manufacture of saleable commodities in favour of art forms which do not lend themselves so easily to such manipulation: for example Conceptual art, Video art, Performance art and Land art.

Given the existential emphasis within Abstract Expressionism, by which every brushmark was judged an authentic sign of the artist's personality and a gesture indicative of his or her free will, it was almost inevitable that subsequent generations would seek a demystification of both process and content as a release from this romantic inwardness. Such impulses were central to the origins of Pop art in the 1950s and to the evolution and influence of the movement in the following decade. Indications of this shift in the late 1950s occurred also in the work of American artists such as Helen Frankenthaler (born 1928) and Morris Louis (1912–62), whose variations on the procedures of Jackson Pollock's drip paintings largely stripped them of their implications as a form of

Philip Guston
The Studio 1969

handwriting conveying emotion; Louis in particular stressed simple actions, such as staining the canvas with rivulets or pools of thinned acrylic paint applied by pouring, to draw attention to the material properties of the painting as a flat surface suffused with colour.

One of Louis's close associates, Kenneth Noland (born 1924), while also favouring acrylic paint stained into rather than brushed on the canvas, introduced into his work a strong formal design as a structuring device for an art of colour and surface. In a number of paintings of the late 1950s and early 1960s he used a target-like motif of concentric rings of colour not as a way of expressing an ironic equivalence between the painting and a real object, as had been the case for Jasper Johns a few years earlier, but as a container for precisely judged relationships of hue; among the diverse precedents for this art of colour and geometry one could thus cite the Orphism of Robert Delaunay and the almost scientifically rigorous *Homage to the Square* paintings of Josef Albers (1888–1976).

Louis, Noland and Frankenthaler, along with other artists such as Frank Stella (born 1936), Ellsworth Kelly (born 1923), Al Held (born 1928) and Jules Olitski (born 1922), were grouped together by the critic Clement Greenberg under the banner of Post-Painterly Abstraction in an exhibition held in 1964. As the label suggests, Greenberg saw in these artists a shared reaction against the importance accorded to painterly gesture in certain types of Abstract Expressionism, arguing their case as a search for the essence of painting as a medium of flat coloured surfaces. Kelly, who was older than most of the artists in this group, had been working independently since the late 1940s on the creation of a concise language of geometric form, initially in painted wooden reliefs inspired by modern architecture; by the early 1960s his preference for clearly outlined brightly coloured shapes led him to being identified as one of the originators of Hard-Edge Painting. Like many labels, this is misleading in its emphasis on a minor technical aspect of the work, as Kelly's concern was not simply with linear definition but with relationships of shape and colour and of self-sufficient form to nature. Another term which is sometimes applied to such work and to that of older American artists such as Barnett Newman and Mark Rothko is Colour Field Painting, which more helpfully emphasizes a shared concern with the effects of saturated hues over a large surface. The proliferation since the 1960s of terms, as of movements, needs to be treated with a certain amount of scepticism: what begins as a useful shorthand for identifying a common purpose may all too quickly degenerate into a restrictive label. Although Post-Painterly Abstraction was destined to remain more a convenient label than a coherent and lasting movement, it did help to define the parameters of much of the art produced during the 1960s: in its elimination of the personal touch as a sign of the artist's personality it heralded the anonymous surfaces of movements as diverse as Pop, Op and Minimal art; in its insistence on logic it set the tone for Conceptual art just as in its concentration on the most basic and essential attributes of painting it prefigured Minimal art; and in its concern with stripping bare the physical properties of each object as the result of a sequence of actions it provided a background for an emphasis on process in the work of other artists later in the decade.

Greenberg's immense influence and single-mindedness as a critic, while doing much to establish the reputations of the American artists he promoted, ultimately undermined the position of those who were judged to be too much under his control, especially when his exclusivity and formalist bias gradually lost favour. The artists whose work continued to develop and to affect the course of art, at least in America, were those who, like Stella and Kelly, had maintained a more independent stance from the beginning. In the late 1950s and early 1960s Stella produced

Frank Stella
Untitled 1962 (?)

1950s and who continued to be regarded as a major international figure
in the grand tradition. Through his teaching at St Martin's School of Art
in London Caro helped redirect the course of sculpture in Britain; among
his former students who came to prominence at the Whitechapel Gallery's
New Generation exhibition in 1965 were Philip King (born 1934), whose
often fanciful variations of geometry were fabricated from industrial
materials including plastic and fibreglass, Tim Scott (born 1937) and
William Tucker (born 1935).

One of the most striking characteristics of Caro's work was his
elimination of the conventional pedestal which had traditionally elevated
sculptures from the environment in which they were sited. The supports
for Caro's constructions were part and parcel of their construction, a
straightforward device through which he was able not only to articulate
the way in which form followed function, as had long been the case in
Modernist architecture, but to seek a more democratic confrontation
between his work and the spectator by acknowledging their interaction
on the same literally down-to-earth level. A similar urge to involve the
viewer directly motivated other tendencies during this period, in
particular Op art and Kinetic art. For Op artists such as the English
Bridget Riley (born 1931), the French Victor Vasarely (born 1908) and
François Morellet (born 1926), the most pressing concern was with the
act of perception itself, with the dazzling and often disorientating effect
on the eyes of particular patterns of line, shape and colour. By definition
such images require the active response of the spectator in order to take
effect. While much Op art depended for its effect on phenomena that had
been more ably investigated by scientists, in the hands of its most
sophisticated practitioners it proved to be far more than a passing fashion
or gimmick in spite of the speed with which it was consumed and imitated
within popular culture in the wake of exhibitions such as *The Responsive
Eye* (held at the Museum of Modern Art, New York) in 1965. Riley, for
instance, followed her purely black and white paintings of 1963 with
canvases of coloured stripes, deployed either as parallel lines or as wave
patterns of alternating thickness, which functioned in many different
ways. In some cases no more than three colours might be juxtaposed in a
variety of configurations in order to create an illusion of an immense
variety of colour by purely optical means involving after-images. Within
the strict limits of her formal vocabulary she was able to continue such
investigations throughout her later work in endless permutations.

Op art is sometimes treated as a branch of Kinetic art, given that both
are concerned with movement: either actual motion, as in Kinetic art, or
implied or imagined action, as in Op art. The dividing line between the
two types can be ambiguous, as in the work of the Venezuelan artist
Jesús-Rafael Soto (born 1923), who is best known for kinetic relief
constructions in which constantly changing patterns are created by the
optical interaction of forms suspended in front of a surface pattern of
parallel lines. The quasi-scientific tone of much of this art can be gleaned
from the very name of the Groupe de Recherche d'Art Visuel, the French
group which during its existence from 1960 to 1968 numbered among its
members Vasarely's son Yvaral (born 1934) and the Argentinian Julio Le
Parc (born 1928). By contrast, however, other Kinetic artists introduced

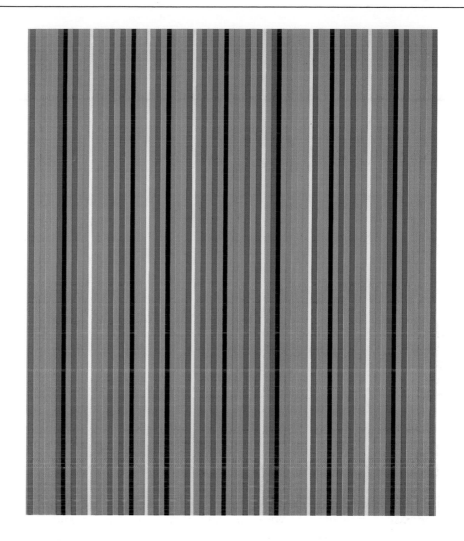

Bridget Riley
Sea Cloud 1981

mystical and absurdist approaches to art in movement: the Greek artist
Takis (born 1925) created eerie musical environments of suspended
metallic objects activated by electromagnetism, while the Swiss Jean
Tinguely (born 1925), a latter-day Dadaist, delighted in creating
unwieldly clattering machines that endlessly repeated patently useless
actions.

A desire for directness of confrontation with the spectator was also one
of the motivating forces in the mid-1960s for the rise of Minimal art, a
movement which stressed simplicity of form and clarity of idea in the
creation of paintings and sculptures as objects that could be apprehended
in their totality virtually at a glance. Paradoxically the very sparseness of
their means, particularly when removed from the defining context of a
group of works conceived as a complete installation, guaranteed the
almost complete incomprehension of the public at large when faced with
works such as Carl Andre's *Equivalent VIII*, a rectangular solid formed by
120 standard bricks stacked in a simple formation in defiance of all

traditional notions of technical skill and composition. Minimal art was taken to its most extreme logical conclusion by certain American sculptors, notably Andre (born 1935), Donald Judd (born 1928) and Dan Flavin (born 1933), who made use of industrial materials, often in readily available prefabricated forms, for a sophisticated art of precise arrangement and interval. Flavin's structural elements, for instance, were fluorescent lights in standard lengths and colours, arranged in basic configurations or simply propped up as a single luminous line as a means of articulating or transforming the space of the room in which they were installed. A heightened awareness of place was essential, too, to the 'floor

Dan Flavin
Untitled 1976

Carl Andre
Aluminium-Copper Alloy Square 1969

pieces' made by Andre from metal plates laid edge-to-edge in a kind of chequerboard pattern, not only because the spectator was encouraged to stand on these works to experience their materiality and a sense of the space they occupied, but also because they were often conceived for particular gallery spaces or installed in such a way as to deflect attention onto the characteristics of the room itself.

Both Frank Stella and Ad Reinhardt, with his dictum that 'Less is more', prefigured and influenced the emphasis on literalness that characterized Minimal art; Reinhardt's 'black paintings' of 1960–66, each of which consisted of an almost invisible cruciform shape imposed on the dark background of a square canvas, were meant to look as much alike as possible so as to prepare the viewer to scrutinize the surface for almost imperceptible variations of hue and tone. With such works an initial impression of immediacy, obviousness and emptiness, further encouraged by their display in series of nearly identical units, often gave way to an appreciation of the extremely subtle variations which occur both within a single painting or sculpture or from one work to the next. In the case of Robert Ryman (born 1930), for instance, every work he has created since the late 1950s could be described blandly as a white painting in a square format, but within these severe restrictions he has explored an immense variety of the properties of the medium: he has used different types of paint, ink and drawing materials (oil, acrylic, gouache, casein, enamel, gesso, emulsion, pastel) on supports ranging from stretched canvas, wood and paper to copper, steel and plexiglass; he has explored changes wrought by scale, different types of brushwork and variations in the relationship of the painted area to the edge; and he has drawn attention to the many ways by which the surface can be fixed to the wall. While

John Chamberlain
Captain O'Hay 1961

sculpture by the English artist Barry Flanagan in 1968, or in the emphasis
on ordinary methods of construction such as folding, tieing, stapling,
stitching and bolting together in paintings by the English artists Richard
Smith and Stephen Buckley (born 1944). For the German-born American
sculptor Eva Hesse (1936–70), the relationship established with the
spectator through this open avowal of the act of making could entail the

Stephen Buckley
Many Angles 1972

Joseph Beuys
Terremoto 1981

Eva Hesse
Sans II 1968

use of transparent materials such as fibreglass, which openly revealed
their structure, and a metaphorical equivalence between organic-looking
pendulous forms and the human body. For Joseph Beuys particular
materials such as felt and fat conveyed an essentially private mythology
rooted in his wartime experiences of protection and survival when near
death; his tendencies towards the esoteric were checked, however, by his

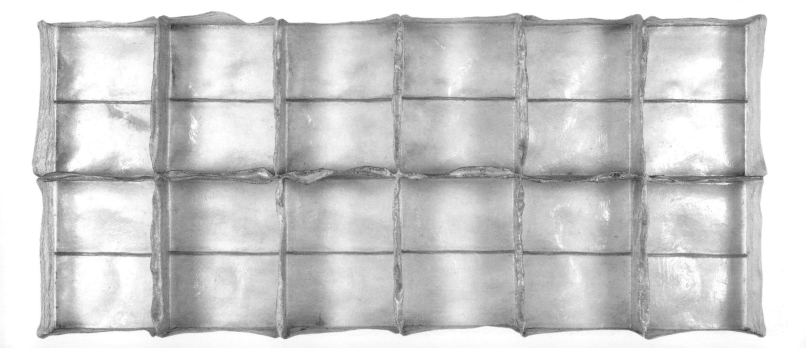

innate sense for the qualities of different materials and for the emotive effects and physical sensations stimulated by sculptures on an environmental scale. One of his last major works, an installation titled *Plight* (1985) at the Anthony d'Offay gallery in London, involved the virtual sealing off of the interior in bundles of felt to create a still, silent, warm and almost claustrophobically sealed shelter or womb-like space. Through such works and occasional performances and lectures Beuys made a strong case for the transcendence of the spirit and of elemental forces over matter, presenting himself as a shaman. Without perhaps ever being fully understood, he remained an immensely influential figure, especially in Germany, for his insistence on art as an instrument capable of healing the wounds of society.

For Beuys and other artists in the 1960s the gallery space was not merely a neutral or passive receptacle for art but an essential part of the art-work itself. The role accorded to presentation by the Minimal artists, for instance, was not simply one of professionalism or commercial astuteness but a means of articulating the meaning of individual works and of their inter-relationships in a specific context; as Barnett Newman had earlier avowed with his term 'hereness', Minimal artists and composers such as Steve Reich and Philip Glass alike sought a concentration of perception and physical being on the immediate moment and thus on the particularity of the place. In the wake of this stress on the exhibition itself as the work of art, artists of diverse stylistic allegiances have placed emphasis on the installation as a whole rather than on its individual components. Environmental art in this specific sense had historical precedents, particularly in pre-Pop works by Claes Oldenburg such as *The Street* (1960) and *The Store* (1961), but what had begun as temporary displays in an almost theatrical context has since become the standard form for artists who otherwise have little in common stylistically or in terms of subject matter. The often mysterious installations by Jannis Kounellis, for example, tend to include traces of the actions by which they came into being, such as the singeing of the gallery walls by smoke. There is little basis on which to relate such works to the highly specific theatrical tableaux created by the American Edward Kienholz (born 1927) or the manifestations of dream imagery produced by a younger

Ed Kienholz
Portable War Memorial 1968

Richard Long
England 1968

American, Jonathan Borofsky (born 1942). For each of them, however, the relationships established within the whole remain of greater importance than the constituent parts.

By the late 1960s such concern with the work of art as a total environment, combined with a desire to remove art from the commercial manipulation and rarefied context of galleries and museums, had helped create the basis of a new art form known as Land art or Earth art. Works by its most notable practitioners, especially in the United States, often occupied a vast space in remote locations and involved the direct interaction of man and nature with the earth itself as a raw sculptural material. Given the vastness of North America and the availability of large stretches of desert and other uninhabited areas of land, it was perhaps inevitable that many of the major artists associated with the movement were American and that their works were often characterized by a grandeur of scale; such was the case with Michael Heizer (born 1944), Dennis Oppenheim (born 1938) and Walter De Maria (born 1935). Other artists, such as the Englishmen Richard Long (born 1945), Hamish Fulton (born 1946) and David Tremlett (born 1945), travelled to places as distant and inhospitable as Greenland and Tibet in search of a suitable location for a communion with nature. The implicit actions performed on the land were often direct and immediate, involving the digging or removal of soil or rock or the restructuring of a site into an elemental and symbolic form such as a spiral, as in works by Robert Smithson (1938–73) such as *Spiral Jetty* (a 1500-foot [457.2-metre] long coil of mud, salt crystals, rock and water at Rozel Point, Great Salt Lake, Utah, 1970) and *Spiral Hill* (a hill at Emmen, Holland, made of earth,

Robert Smithson
Spiral Hill, Emmen 1971

black topsoil and white sand, measuring approximately 75 feet [22.8 metres] at its base, executed in 1971). The forms taken by Land art could involve nothing more than the subtle relocation of natural elements indicating the passage of a human being through a hitherto untouched environment, as in works by Richard Long such as *England* (1968), which consisted of a large X shape made on a grassy field by the removal of the heads of daisies; these works, documented in photographs, were temporary by definition, since the cycles of mortality at work in nature were built into their very structure. In this type of art it was often the case that the direct experience was afforded only to the artist himself, and it was left to the spectator's imagination to reconstruct its physical character by means of photographs, maps and written documentation of a sometimes overtly poetic nature, as in the work of Hamish Fulton. Long also produced works for installation in galleries, particularly floor pieces which bore some formal resemblance to the Minimal art of Andre but which made a specific connection through their materials – quantities of stone or driftwood – to specific natural locations as a way of connecting the two environments and the experiences which they represent. The preoccupations of other Land artists, particularly in the United States, were more overtly sculptural in a traditional sense, as in works by the Bulgarian-born artist Christo (born 1935) such as *Wrapped Coast* (Sydney, Australia, 1969) and *Valley Curtain* (Colorado, 1971), in which the shape and mass of large areas of land were articulated by massive quantities of cloth.

If much Land art indicated a nostalgic desire for an escape from civilization as well as from the corruption of art by its commercial exploitation, similar motivations encouraged the development of another art form during the 1960s: Performance art. Although its origins can be

Christo
Wrapped Coast – Little Bay, Australia 1969

traced to theatrical provocations early in the century by Futurists, Russian Constructivists, Dadaists, Surrealists and other Modernist artists, it was in the late 1950s that it began to take shape more explicitly as a means of making art in its own right, for example in the Happenings by New York artists associated with the origins of Pop art such as Allan Kaprow (born 1927), Claes Oldenburg, Jim Dine (born 1935), Red Grooms (born 1937), Robert Whitman (born 1935) and Robert Rauschenberg. Performances could be gruelling experiences for the artist and audience alike, both physically and intellectually, as in works by Joseph Beuys such as *How to Explain Pictures to a Dead Hare* and *Twenty-four Hours* (both 1965), which demanded high levels of concentration and physical stamina as part of their confrontational nature and examination of consciousness. Feats of endurance and physical pain, to which especially Europeans such as Hermann Nitsch (born 1938), Günter Brus (born 1938), Arnulf Rainer (born 1929), Gina Pane (born 1939) and Stuart Brisley (born 1933) subjected their bodies, often had ritualistic and

Stuart Brisley
And for Today – Nothing 1972

Robert Wilson
Still from *Einstein on the Beach* 1976

expressionist overtones as part of a purging of social or religious patterns
of behaviour. Artists associated with Body art, such as the Americans
Scott Burton and Lucinda Childs, used the human figure as a sculptural
element as part of a contemplation of time and space, while for others
such as the Canadian group General Idea (formed in 1968 by A. A.
Bronson, Felix Partz and Jorge Zontal), the British team of Gilbert and
George (born 1943 and 1942) and the Scottish artist Bruce McLean
(born 1944) doses of humour and vaudeville provided a means of
unmasking human behaviour and the pretensions of the art world.
Performances could be improvised and spontaneous or as intricately
scripted and visually exacting as the ambitious theatrical events staged by
the American Robert Wilson (born 1941), such as his collaboration with
the composer Philip Glass on the opera *Einstein on the Beach* (1976).
Performance art, in other words, while never achieving a very wide
public, proved to be as flexible and various as any art form in the styles,
moods and themes which it was able to convey. The ephemerality and
lack of marketability which had initially attracted many artists to such
work, however, in the end contributed to the marginalization of the form,
and many of those associated with it turned again to the production of
more conventional art objects as sculptors or painters.

Performance art, while particularly lucid in its emphasis on action in
time rather than on the creation of a finite object, was only one of several
media which challenged traditional artistic priorities during this period.
The Video art initiated early in the 1960s by the Korean Nam Jun Paik
(born 1932) and others, while dependent on the physical sensations
afforded by the latest technology, used television sets not as ends in
themselves but as a means of transmitting a specifically contemporary
experience of the modern world or of recording for posterity an otherwise
transient performance. For Paik in particular the medium offered a
suitable means of expressing and questioning the bombardment of the
senses effected by the mass media. All such moves away from standard

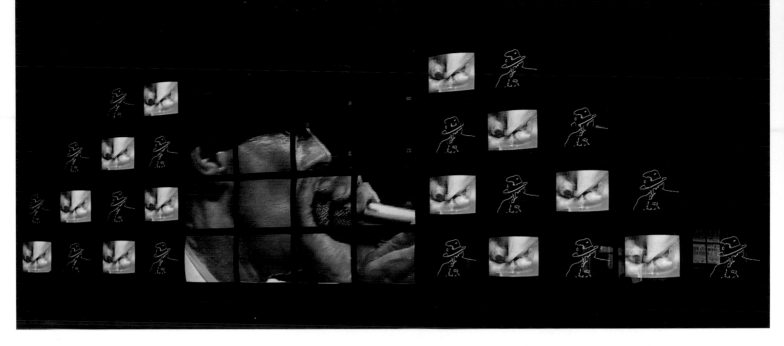

Nam Jun Paik
Beuys-Voice 1987

media, including Process art, Land art and Performance art, presaged a general emphasis in the later 1960s away from the object in favour of the generating idea. In its most extreme form, Conceptual art, the idea alone could be presented as the work of art. In an essay titled 'Art After Philosophy', published in *Studio International* in October 1969, the leading American exponent of Conceptual art, Joseph Kosuth (born 1945), cited Marcel Duchamp's invention of the 'unassisted Ready-made' as the single event which changed the focus of art from 'appearance' to 'conception', 'from the form of the language to what was being said'. Kosuth's own work often relied on photographic enlargements of dictionary definitions

Joseph Kosuth
One and Three Chairs 1965

Marcel Broodthaers
La Salle Blanche 1975

presented as equivalents to real objects or to their representations in
photographs. Much of Conceptual art was text-based, with the written
word functioning as a replacement for visual signs, as in the handpainted
phrases presented on gallery walls by the American Lawrence Weiner
(born 1940); while much of this type of art was pedantically and
ponderously intellectual, Weiner continued in his later works to use words
for their visual suggestiveness, as in *BILLOWING CLOUDS OF
FERROUS OXIDE SETTING APART A CORNER ON THE BOTTOM
OF THE SEA* (1986), in the process making a strong case for the power
of language and memory in conveying experience. Another artist who
relished paradoxical interchanges between words, objects and images was
the Belgian Marcel Broodthaers (1924–76), whose Conceptualism was at
least partly rooted in the paradoxes of the Surrealist René Magritte; for
example in an installation titled *La Salle Blanche* (1975) he reconstructed
in wood the surfaces of two rooms in his house on which he had inscribed
references both to standard images in painting (shadow, sunlight, clouds)
and to things used in the making and promotion of art (canvas, easel,
gallery, percentage, museum).

Conceptual art, in spite of its apparent affront to the marketing of art
objects, was severely dependent on its context in order to express its
meaning; outside a gallery or museum it ran the risk of failing to be
recognized as art. The leading French Conceptual artist, Daniel Buren
(born 1938), turned this situation into a virtue by basing his work on the
changes wrought by different environments to a single visual sign – a
simple pattern of alternating stripes – which through constant use was
paradoxically transformed from an anonymous image into his personal
trademark. It was through words, however, that most Conceptual artists
conveyed their ideas; one of the most active groups, Art and Language,

A PROMISE OF TRADITION
You mustn't be too hard on them.
So many things to cope with. So much to do.
They keep rabbits. They keep house.
They keep up appearances.
If they fail to keep their word
you must excuse them. They're good people.
Almost all of them. They may not see you.
They may not hear you. They may not want to.
It's not their fault. They mean well.
They have promised to try again.

Victor Burgin
A Promise of Tradition 1976

Barbara Kruger
'Untitled' (I Shop Therefore I Am) 1987

Daniel Buren
Les Deux Plateaux 1986

even published its own magazine as a forum for its British and American members. In England a variant of Conceptual art dependent on the relationships established between written texts and photographic images provided the structure for philosophical, social and political enquiry; among the practitioners of this type of art were Victor Burgin (born 1941), John Stezaker (born 1949) and Stephen Willats (born 1943). In the 1980s two Americans, Barbara Kruger (born 1945) and Jenny Holzer (born 1950), were among those who even more explicitly sought to decode the methods of advertising and the mass media in order to reverse

Malcolm Morley
SS Amsterdam in Front of Rotterdam 1966

the depersonalization and manipulation to which they generally subjected viewers assumed to be passive consumers.

In its most extreme forms Conceptual art was perhaps ultimately too rarefied to be effective as an antidote to object-based art, but in retrospect virtually every ambitious form of art proposed since the 1960s has made its case on a central defining idea. On first sight nothing could seem further from the intellectual thrust of Conceptual art than the apparently unquestioning imitation of photographic forms of representation by the painters and sculptors associated with another movement of the same period, Photorealism. Painters such as the English-born Malcolm Morley (born 1931) and the Americans Richard Estes (born 1936), Robert Cottingham (born 1935) and Robert Bechtle (born 1932), however, were not concerned simply with replicating the appearance of a snapshot as a technical *tour-de-force*; their presentation of the canvas as a found object was a philosophical gesture that would have been unthinkable without the example of Duchamp, and their obsessive concern with equating the vision of eye and camera was a means of addressing issues of mimesis and perception which had challenged the thinking of artists for centuries. Photorealism was largely an American

Richard Estes
Paris Street-Scene 1973

movement, and like the Pop art which served as one of its sources it was often interpreted in terms of its subject matter either as a critique or a celebration of lowbrow suburban culture. In its very dependence on readymade imagery, however, it declared its detachment and non-judgmental scrutiny. Even in the life-size sculptural figures by John De Andrea (born 1941) and especially Duane Hanson (born 1925), the narrative social connotations which sometimes threaten to engulf the image in kitsch remain subservient to the physical presence and shock of recognition occasioned by the apparent fidelity to appearances.

Duane Hanson
Tourists 1970

While Photorealism was popular with collectors and with the general public for its virtuosity and clarity of imagery, it proved short-lived as a movement among both critics and other artists. Although initially promoted as a return to figuration, by definition it held no real possibility of development apart from that of technique for its own sake, since the artist could aspire to nothing more than the duplication of evidence much more easily amassed by the camera. By 1971 Morley had adopted frenetically expressionist brushwork and violent gestures of fragmentation in deliberate subversion of the cool neutrality of his earlier paintings. Given the Photorealists' apparent lack of subjective involvement in the act of picturing, any distinction drawn between abstraction and representation was beginning to seem meaningless in any case. If it was an immediate source of imagery that was required, why not simply use photographs? Such seems to have been the conclusion reached by Gilbert and George, the self-styled 'Living Sculptures' who had made their name as performance artists, when they turned in the mid-1970s to the

Gilbert and George
Sleepy 1985

production of composite photographic images in which they presented themselves in the context of emblems of their emotions, perceptions and experiences. For the American Cindy Sherman (born 1954), too, photographs for which she always served as the model provided a direct measure of contrasting notions of identity, self-image and gender; the explicit appropriation of the presentation methods of film-stills in her first black-and-white and colour photographs of the late 1970s and early 1980s soon gave way to a greater reliance on her own ability to transform herself into different characters through gestures and changes in her appearance. It was, however, another American photographer, Duane Michals (born 1932), who from the late 1960s most eloquently used the medium to convey thoughts about mortality, desire, loneliness and vulnerability. Although he was widely influential for his formal innovations, such as the use of serial imagery for narrative purposes or the pairing of images with handwritten texts, it was in introducing an intimacy of tone that he made his most courageous and welcome inroads into the largely public sphere of contemporary art.

By the early 1970s a number of painters, too, were making a strong case not only for the continuing validity of their medium but for the subjectivity of a one-to-one relationship with subject and spectator alike. One of the most reticent of the Abstract Expressionists of the 1950s, Philip Guston (1913–80), shocked many of his former supporters when he turned in the late 1960s to an overtly representational style of almost cartoon-like vulgarity as a means of dealing unflinchingly with the circumstances of his studio existence and with passing thoughts, anxieties,

Cindy Sherman
Untitled no. 98 1982

Duane Michals
The Unfortunate Man 1976

THE UNFORTUNATE MAN

The unfortunate man could not touch the one he loved.
It had been declared illegal by the government.
Slowly his fingers became toes, and his hands became
feet. He began to wear shoes on his hands to hide his shame.
It never occurred to him to break the law.

memories and sensations. The generosity of spirit in his work, the insistence on art as a reflection of the fullness of his attitudes about life, presaged much of the painting that was to emerge towards the end of the 1970s from the studios of much younger artists. He was not alone, however, in resisting the purely formal and materialist notions of painting which had been so vigorously promoted in the 1960s by critics such as Clement Greenberg. Since the late 1940s in England Francis Bacon had steadfastly maintained his ambition to create figure inventions of such physical immediacy and energy as to appear to emanate, as he explained, from his nervous system. His work was a particular inspiration to other painters working in Britain, including Leon Kossoff (born 1926) and two German-born artists, Frank Auerbach (born 1931) and Lucian Freud (born 1922), for each of whom the physical substance of the painting was a direct materialization of the subject, often another human being painted from life. For Auerbach each painting exemplified a constant process of forming an image, scraping it down and then reconstituting it until it corresponded in form, texture, weight, tone and colour to his sense of the subject it represented; the accretion of paint, sometimes of such density and thickness as to risk incoherence, itself became a sign for the labour and time involved in the production of the image. In Freud's case

Frank Auerbach
*Looking towards Mornington Crescent Station,
Night* 1972–73

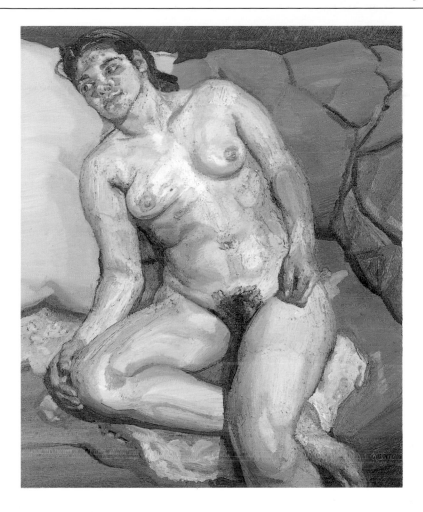

Lucian Freud
Esther 1980

the calculated application of each brush-stroke in conjuring a human presence functioned both as evidence of his obsessive scrutiny of the subject and as a material counterpart for the suppleness of human flesh. Such concern with what the art historian Irving Sandler has termed 'perceptual realism' also motivated painters of the human figure in other countries, notably the American Philip Pearlstein (born 1924), whose clarity of form and accuracy of detail were sometimes misleadingly associated with Photorealism.

The openly traditional goals of such painters of the human figure lent increasing weight in the 1970s to those who questioned the pre-eminence still accorded the avant-garde for its own sake. For the Paris-based Israeli artist Avigdor Arikha (born 1929), for example, truth of expression had to reside in the particularities of working directly from the motif or from the human figure, as had been the case for artists from Velázquez through to Degas and Vuillard. Why, indeed, should such directness be deemed to have run its course simply because it failed to correspond to Modernism's insistence on the invention of new forms? Even in his

Avigdor Arikha
August 1982

paintings of empty interiors Arikha was intent on conveying, through the quivering presence of each brush-stroke, a palpably physical sensation of stillness and the comforting warmth of light. For the London-based American R. B. Kitaj (born 1932), who in the 1960s had unwittingly influenced the course of Pop art, such pre-Modernist traditions of life drawing had also become the most rigorous standard of excellence. His most ambitious paintings, however, combined Modernist principles of juxtaposition derived from Surrealism and collage with a concept of

R. B. Kitaj
The Autumn of Central Paris (After Walter Benjamin) 1972–73

Georg Baselitz
Waldarbeiter 1968

allegory rooted in Renaissance and Symbolist art, with images chosen for
their layering of meaning through re-use, as in the art historical discipline
of iconology. Often misguidedly accused of eclecticism, Kitaj in fact made
a powerful case for the availability to modern artists of the entire fund of
historical styles and images. Kitaj's work presaged the development of
many younger artists not just in his commitment to representation but to
passionate convictions about particular themes and to a freewheeling
synthesis of separate elements filtered through one artist's sensibility and
related to a coherent subject matter.

   In Germany as early as the 1960s a number of artists such as Georg
Baselitz (born 1938) and A. R. Penck (born 1939), both originally from
East Germany, had sought to fragment and overturn conventions of
painting in search of a vitality and violence which had specific precedents
in turn-of-the-century Expressionism. In his early work Baselitz favoured

Anselm Kiefer
Die Meistersinger 1982

Francesco Clemente
Interior Landscape 1980

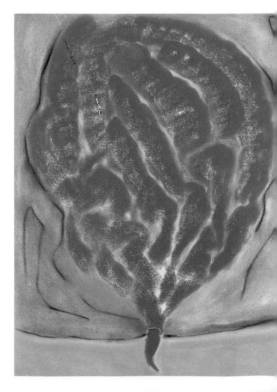

(born 1950) and Mimmo Paladino (born 1948). Promoted under various labels, including the Transavanguardia and New Image painting, they made frequent reference to their place in Modernist traditions – for example in Chia's case by allusions to an earlier Italian movement, Futurism – while stressing their inherent subjectivity and their elevation of the imagination over intellect. Among Clemente's most affecting works were small-scale, lusciously coloured and sensual pastel drawings conceived as emblematic representations of the human body. Like many of the New Image painters, however, he made a point of working in a large variety of styles and media as if bound to express the restlessness of his visual life and to define his complex relationships to conflicting traditions originating in different cultures and periods. Through such thinking a series of overtly Expressionist oil paintings such as *The Fourteen Stations* (1982), in which he reinterpreted a symbolically laden Christian theme by means of his own recurring image, could co-exist with large-scale gouaches on paper in which he transformed his appreciation of Indian miniatures into a poignantly awkward archaic style, as if he were reinventing conventions of representation. For other Italian artists such as Cucchi, as for Beuys in Germany, the emphasis lay largely in defining the role of the artist as visionary; in Cucchi's case images with ritualistic overtones are often conveyed in sombre and emotive colours and with an impassioned brushwork indicative of an all-consuming energy. As he explained in a brief text in 1979, 'One can establish profound things in the material components of the work. They say it is useless to reason with

Enzo Cucchi
A Painting of Precious Fires
1983

the head. Then we'll reason with the elbow (again), but only when we quicken our "rhythm" step.' Logic and material fact were no longer such attractive propositions to many artists, perhaps specifically because of the sway that these characteristics had held throughout much of the 1960s and 1970s. Peter Phillips (born 1939), for example, who from 1960 had

Peter Phillips
Anvil of the Heart 1986

seemed one of the most rigorous and defiantly materialistic Pop painters in Britain, turned in the late 1970s to a mysterious dream-like imagery in paintings of extreme refinement and delicacy. He continued to base his pictures on collages of photographic images culled from magazines but presented them now as fragments of obscure origin rather than as immediately recognizable images. Familiar in their texture but naggingly unidentifiable in form, such motifs appeal to the spectator's memory and to sensations of touch as a means of short-circuiting a self-consciously cerebral response.

A number of artists in the 1980s have addressed themselves to the virtual impossibility of originality given the sheer weight of innovation presented in the many guises of Modernism for nearly a century. Rather than wage what might seem to be a losing battle, artists such as the

Sigmar Polke
The Copyist 1982

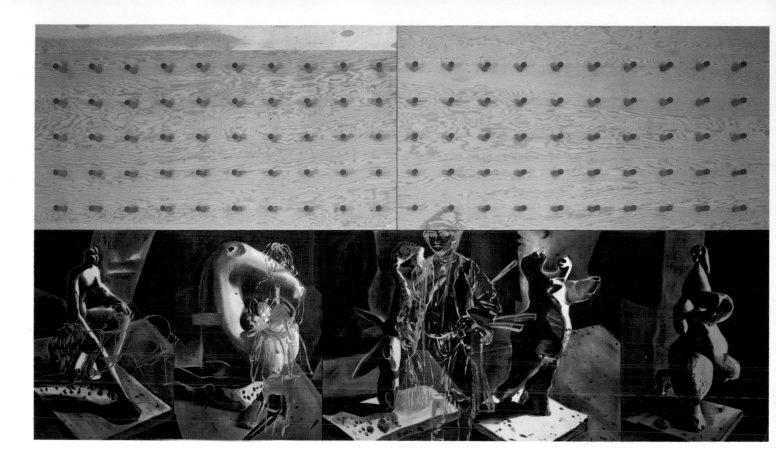

David Salle
My Head 1984

Germans Sigmar Polke (born 1941) and the Czechoslovakian-born Jiři Georg Dokoupil (born 1954), the American David Salle (born 1952) and the Japanese Shinro Ohtake (born 1955) have chosen to embrace as many different styles and methods of working as possible, either from picture to picture or even in a profusion of seemingly contradictory idioms within a single canvas. Motivated to a large measure by the detachment towards style demonstrated in the 1960s in Pop art, and even earlier by the assertion of the Dadaist Francis Picabia that styles should be changed with the same frequency as one's shirt, such forms of representation could best be apprehended as conceptual acts. In such works intentions are often left deliberately ambiguous. Is Polke's presumed self-image as a copyist an emblem of despair and cynicism, for example, or one of exhilaration at the prospect of devouring and making one's own something which is already in existence? Should we assume from Salle's *My Head* that he is mocking the obtuseness or congestion of his imagination or celebrating the wealth of images teeming within it? For Ohtake as a young Japanese artist the predicament has specific cultural connotations in the hunger to assimilate and paraphrase every conceivable variety of contemporary Western art so as to restate it in his own terms.

One of the words most often cited by young artists in the 1980s was *appropriation*. This could entail the emulation by New York painters such as Jean-Michel Basquiat (1960–88) and Keith Haring (1958–90) of the urgent street culture represented by the graffiti scrawled on walls or subway trains, or acts of such Duchampian simplicity as the presentation

Shinro Ohtake
Family Tree 1986–88

Jeff Koons
Rabbit 1986

by the American Jeff Koons (born 1955) of a sculpture cast in stainless
steel from a bargain-shop Easter rabbit. In a similar spirit another
American, Sherrie Levine (born 1947), had earlier displayed as her own
work framed photographic reproductions of famous modern paintings.
She wrote in 1981: 'The world is filled to suffocating. Man has placed his
token on every stone. Every word, every image, is leased and mortgaged.
. . . Succeeding the painter, the plagiarist no longer bears within him
passions, humours, feelings, impressions, but rather this immense
encyclopaedia from which he draws.' For another American, Julian
Schnabel (born 1951), the answer lay not in acquiescence but in an often
violent assault on his chosen images and materials alike; in his best-known
works, painted on a jagged surface of broken crockery, he seemed intent
on literally destroying all conventions by a sheer act of will. As in the art
of earlier Modernists, there is a sense that everything is possible and that
art can be made out of whatever materials, images and subjects are most
readily to hand, yet the optimism with which such methods had
previously been associated seems unavoidably weighted now with the

Jean-Michel Basquiat/Andy Warhol
Collaboration 1984

Sherrie Levine
Untitled (Lead Checks 6) 1987

Julian Schnabel
The Death of Fashion 1978

demands of career, competition and ego. Others, however, have suggested ways in which apparently unconstrained appropriation can serve to create a dialogue between different levels of experience and society. For example the English painter Colin Self (born 1941), best known for his intense and unsettling Pop art drawings of the 1960s, has demonstrated in collage paintings a readiness to make his own not just styles but actual artefacts produced by others as a way of exploring our common humanity. In '*Let's have it here and charge admission . . .*' (1988) he has appended mass-produced plastic toys (including a figure of the comic strip character Bugs Bunny) to an amateur Tachist painting of the type produced in evening classes; the casual, almost throwaway quality of this act belies, however, Self's deeply held convictions about what he calls 'people's art' as a form of artistic expression worthy of our respect.

Colin Self
Let's have it Here and Charge Admission . . .
1988

Against such currents of stylistic manipulation during the 1980s, other painters have sought to use their work as a vehicle for human psychology. The American Eric Fischl (born 1948) has specialized in narratives of the seamier side of suburban life, in which larger-than-life and often naked human figures are encountered in intimate and sexually charged situations that turn us uncomfortably into voyeurs. Although the images are clearly derived from photographs, our attention is deflected from their probable source to their materialization as succulent paint and then to the significance of their gestures and inter-relationships in the drama of an otherwise unexplained moment. Although similar subject matter had

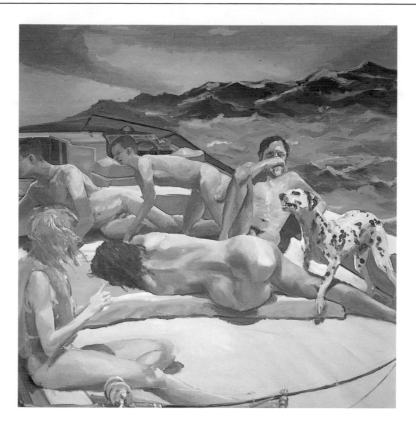

Eric Fischl
The Old Man's Boat and the Old Man's Dog
1982

been explored by the French painter Balthus (born 1908) since the 1930s in his erotic presentation of young women in claustrophobic interiors, or in the English painter David Hockney's (born 1937) large double portraits of the late 1960s, which were subtly expressive of isolation and mutual dependence, the possibilities for other painters were far from exhausted. Paula Rego (born 1935), a Portuguese-born artist resident in

Paula Rego
The Maids 1987

England, began in the mid-1980s to make specific reference to childhood memories resurrected almost in the manner of theatrical tableaux by means of a persuasively volumetric treatment of objects in space; however innocent the actions of the figures might at first appear, a disturbing sense remains of sado-masochistic power and dependence. In many of Hockney's paintings of the 1980s the human figure is no longer directly represented; by means, however, of pictorial devices such as multiple viewpoints and reverse perspective, interior spaces are organized so that we as spectators have taken centre stage in an overt acknowledgment of our presence and of our role in completing the picture.

Abstraction and representation, terms which seemed to define irreconcilable positions at the start of the 1960s, no longer hold much meaning in the work of many artists. The English painter Howard Hodgkin (born 1932), for instance, has relied largely on a severe vocabulary of simple brushmarks and basic geometric forms, but his layering of the surface with coloured patterns has a specific function in each case in reconstituting the memory of a person or group of people in a particular location, often an interior space. In that sense his work, while it uses a language resembling abstraction, remains an intimate art of human behaviour and emotion. For the German painter Gerhard Richter (born 1932), by contrast, a dependence on the photograph as a mediator since his Pop work of the 1960s has served to draw attention to the

David Hockney
Large Interior, Los Angeles 1988

Opposite:

Howard Hodgkin
Dinner at Smith Square c. 1978–79

Gerhard Richter
Sulphur 1985

Bill Woodrow
Twin-Tub with Beaver 1981

identity of every image both as an abstraction and as a representation.
His landscapes represent not so much a specific place as their
photographic source, and in that sense remain conceptual acts; conversely
his 'abstract' paintings, possessed of illusions of photographic variations of
focus in their contrasts between crisp delineation and smudginess, read as
representations of brush-strokes rather than simply as studies in form.

Such interplays between reality and illusion, between the work of art as
a thing in itself and as a sign for another level of experience, were central
to much art of the 1980s. It was to such ends that a number of British
sculptors, including Tony Cragg (born 1949) and Bill Woodrow (born
1948), used as their basic material found objects, sometimes altered but
presented without disguise. A work by Cragg such as *Plastic Palette II*
(1985), formed as the title indicates not from paint but from individual
shards of cheap plastic, may at first appear to be a caustic comment
about a now outmoded concept of what it means to be an artist. As an
emblem of his own definition of creativity, however, it is as lucid as it is
sincere: for what he presents to us here, in a mood of celebration, are his
raw materials transformed into art, all the more to be cherished because
they had been abandoned as useless by others. Woodrow's inventive

fabrication of metaphoric images from discarded consumer items, their
original identity still clearly visible, likewise presents the artist's duty as
one of salvaging and making new, as is explicitly the case with *Twin-tub
with Beaver* (1981).

Almost every movement and art form initiated since the early 1960s
continues to exist as a defensible proposition as we approach the last
decade of the century. Styles have appeared to succeed each other like
passing fashions, with conflicting impulses and alternative traditions
defended with equal vehemence and conviction. No single way of working
can be said any longer to dominate, as had been the case earlier in the
century. Unnerving as it may be to feel the ground constantly shifting
under our feet, it can safely be said that not since the advent of
Modernism at the end of the nineteenth century have artists been faced
with such an openness and wealth of possibilities.

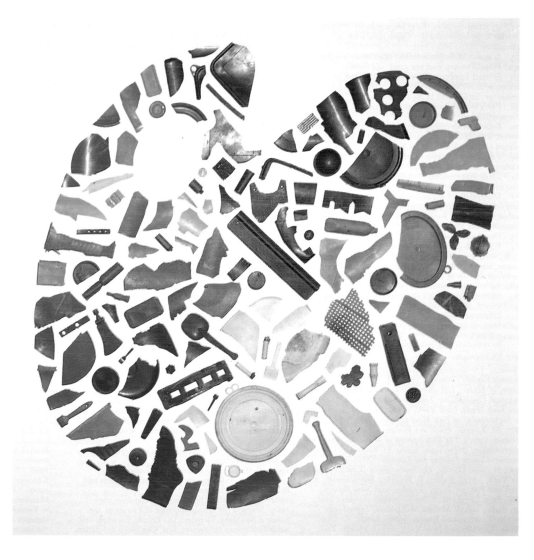

Tony Cragg
Plastic Palette II 1985

Illustration Credits

Index